Bank Statement Mortgage Loans for Self-Employed Borrowers

How Entrepreneurs Qualify for Mortgage Loans Without Traditional Income

By Joseph G. Correa

Licensed Mortgage Broker, Finibi Mortgage

Copyright & Legal Notice

Published by Live Stronger Faster

The information provided in this book is for educational and informational purposes only and does not constitute financial, legal, tax, or investment advice. Although the author is a licensed mortgage professional, the content presented is general in nature and is not intended as personalized guidance for any specific individual or financial situation.

The strategies, structuring methods, and examples discussed in this book are illustrative and educational in nature. They are intended to demonstrate concepts related to bank statement mortgage loan qualification and structuring, including deposit analysis, expense ratio application, and investor guideline interpretation. These examples do not represent guaranteed outcomes or approvals. Results may vary significantly based on individual financial profiles, documentation, credit history, property type, and lender-specific requirements.

First Edition, 2026

Table of Contents

Introduction

The path to homeownership and real estate investing has never been more complex—or more misunderstood—for self-employed borrowers. Entrepreneurs, business owners, freelancers, and independent contractors represent one of the fastest-growing segments of the workforce, yet they are often the most underserved when it comes to traditional mortgage financing. While their income may be strong, scalable, and even far greater than that of salaried employees, the way it is documented often creates barriers in conventional underwriting systems that rely heavily on tax returns. This disconnect has led many highly capable borrowers to believe they cannot qualify for a mortgage when, in reality, they simply need a different approach. That is where bank statement mortgage loans become a powerful and transformative solution.

This book is designed specifically for self-employed individuals who want to take control of their financing options and understand how to present their income in a way that aligns with how lenders actually evaluate risk. Unlike traditional mortgage programs that focus on net income after deductions, bank statement loans shift the focus to cash flow—what is actually coming into your accounts and how consistently it is being generated. For entrepreneurs who strategically use tax deductions to minimize taxable income, this distinction is critical. What may appear as low income on paper could, in fact, represent a highly profitable and sustainable business when viewed through the lens of deposits and revenue trends.

As a self-employed borrower, you operate in a world where income is rarely linear. Some months may be significantly stronger than others. Revenue may come in waves, tied to contracts, projects, or seasonal demand. Expenses may fluctuate depending on growth strategies, reinvestment decisions, or operational needs. Traditional underwriting models often struggle to interpret this variability, but bank statement programs are specifically designed to account for it. They recognize that income stability does not always mean identical monthly earnings—it means consistent overall performance over time. This book will teach you how to frame that performance in a way that makes sense to lenders and increases your chances of approval.

One of the most important concepts you will learn is how to structure your financial profile before you even apply for a loan. Mortgage approval is not just about what you have already done; it is also about how you prepare. The way you manage your bank accounts, categorize your deposits, and control your expenses can significantly impact how your income is calculated. For example, commingling personal and business funds can create confusion and reduce clarity for underwriters. On the other hand, clean, well-organized accounts can make your file stronger, more transparent, and easier to approve. Throughout this book, you will discover practical strategies to optimize your financial presentation without changing the fundamentals of your business.

Another key area of focus is understanding how lenders apply expense ratios when analyzing bank statements. Because business deposits do not equal net profit, lenders must estimate expenses to determine qualifying income. This is often done using standardized expense factors or, in some cases, CPA-prepared profit and loss statements. Knowing how these calculations work—and how to position your business within them—can make a substantial difference in your loan eligibility. You will learn when it is advantageous to use bank statements alone and when a CPA-prepared P&L can strengthen your file by providing a more accurate picture of your profitability.

Reducing red flags in underwriting is another essential component of success. Many self-employed borrowers are denied not because they lack income, but because their financial documentation raises questions. Large unexplained deposits, irregular transfer patterns, declining revenue trends, or excessive expense assumptions can all create hesitation for lenders. This book will guide you through the most common red flags and show you how to proactively address them. By understanding what underwriters look for, you can take steps to eliminate uncertainty and present a clear, compelling case for approval.

Documentation strategy is also critical. Unlike traditional borrowers who rely on W-2s and pay stubs, self-employed individuals must provide a different set of documents to verify income and business stability. This may include bank statements, business licenses, letters from CPAs, and other supporting materials. Knowing exactly what to provide—and how to present it—can streamline the approval process and reduce delays. You will learn how to build a complete and professional loan file that meets lender requirements and demonstrates the strength of your business.

Beyond the technical aspects, this book also addresses the mindset shift required to succeed as a self-employed borrower in the mortgage world. Too often, entrepreneurs approach the process with frustration or skepticism, believing that the system is stacked against them. While it is true that traditional guidelines were not built with self-employed income in mind, alternative programs like bank statement loans have opened new doors. By understanding the rules of these programs and learning how to work within them, you can turn what once felt like a disadvantage into a strategic advantage.

It is also important to recognize that not all lenders and investors evaluate bank statement loans in the same way. Guidelines can vary, including how income is calculated, what expense ratios are used, and what compensating factors are required. This means that structuring your loan is not just about meeting minimum requirements—it is about aligning your profile with the right lender. In this book, you will gain insight into how different investor guidelines work and how to position yourself for the best possible outcome. This knowledge can help you avoid unnecessary denials and identify opportunities that others might overlook.

As you move through this book, you will begin to see that qualifying for a mortgage as a self-employed borrower is not about fitting into a rigid system—it is about understanding how to present your financial story in a way that makes sense to lenders. Every deposit, every expense, and every document contributes to that story. When structured correctly, it can demonstrate not only your ability to repay a loan but also the strength and resilience of your business. This is especially important in today's lending environment, where flexibility exists, but clarity is still essential.

Whether your goal is to purchase a primary residence, invest in real estate, or refinance an existing property, the principles in this book will provide a foundation for success. You will learn how to take control of your financial narrative, reduce uncertainty in your loan file, and position yourself as a strong and qualified borrower. More importantly, you will gain confidence in your ability to navigate the mortgage process as an entrepreneur, knowing that your income—when properly understood and presented—is just as valid and powerful as any traditional paycheck.

This book is not just about getting approved for a mortgage; it is about unlocking opportunities. For many self-employed individuals, access to financing is the key to scaling their investments, improving their living situation, or achieving long-term financial goals. By mastering the strategies outlined here, you can move beyond the limitations of traditional income documentation and embrace a system that works with you, not against you. The journey begins with understanding—and that is exactly what this book is here to provide.

Chapter 1

Understanding Self-Employed Income in Mortgage Underwriting

Self-employed borrowers operate in a financial world that is fundamentally different from that of traditional W-2 employees, and this difference is at the core of why mortgage qualification can feel so challenging. When a salaried employee applies for a mortgage, the process is relatively straightforward: lenders review pay stubs, W-2 forms, and employment history to confirm stable and predictable income. For a self-employed borrower, however, income is not defined by a fixed paycheck but by the performance of a business. This performance is reflected in deposits, revenue streams, expenses, and profit margins, all of which must be interpreted through a different lens. Understanding how lenders view this type of income is the first and most important step toward achieving approval.

The key distinction lies in how income is calculated. Traditional underwriting relies heavily on tax returns, focusing on net income after deductions. For self-employed individuals, this often creates a disadvantage because tax strategies are typically designed to minimize taxable income. Business owners deduct expenses such as equipment, travel, marketing, and operational costs to reduce their tax burden. While this is beneficial from a tax perspective, it can significantly lower the income figure that lenders use when evaluating a mortgage application. As a result, a borrower who generates substantial revenue may appear to have insufficient income on paper, leading to denial under conventional guidelines.

Bank statement mortgage loans were created to address this gap by shifting the focus from net income to cash flow. Instead of relying solely on tax returns, lenders analyze deposits into personal or business bank accounts over a 12- or 24-month period. These deposits provide a clearer picture of the borrower's actual earnings and business activity. For self-employed borrowers, this approach aligns more closely with reality, as it captures the full scope of income before deductions are applied. However, it also introduces new considerations, such as how deposits are categorized, how expenses are estimated, and how consistency is evaluated over time.

Consistency is one of the most critical factors in underwriting self-employed income. Lenders are not just looking for high earnings; they are looking for stability. This means that income should demonstrate a pattern of reliability, even if it fluctuates from month to month. For example, a borrower who earns $10,000 one month and $20,000 the next may still be considered stable if the overall trend shows consistent or increasing revenue. On the other hand, a borrower with declining deposits over time may raise concerns, even if the total income is relatively high. Understanding how to present consistent performance is essential for building a strong loan file.

Another important aspect is the distinction between gross deposits and qualifying income. While bank statements show total deposits, lenders must account for business expenses to determine how much of that income is available to repay a mortgage. This is typically done using an expense ratio, which represents the percentage of revenue assumed to be spent on business operations. For example, if a lender applies a 50% expense ratio to $20,000 in monthly deposits, the qualifying income would be $10,000. This adjustment ensures that the income used for qualification reflects the borrower's actual financial capacity rather than total revenue alone.

The type of bank account used also plays a significant role in how income is evaluated. Personal bank statements are often used for sole proprietors or individuals who receive income directly, while business bank statements are used for companies with separate accounts. Each type has its own considerations. Personal accounts may require careful analysis to separate business income from personal transfers, while business accounts may involve higher expense ratios due to operational costs. Choosing the right approach depends on the structure of the borrower's business and how income flows through their accounts.

Documentation is another critical component of the process. Self-employed borrowers must provide clear and complete records to support their income claims. This includes bank statements, business licenses, and sometimes letters from accountants or CPAs. The goal is to create a transparent and verifiable picture of the borrower's financial situation. Any gaps or inconsistencies in documentation can lead to delays or denials, making it essential to prepare thoroughly before applying for a loan.

One of the most common challenges for self-employed borrowers is the presence of red flags in their financial records. These may include large unexplained deposits, frequent transfers between accounts, or irregular income patterns. While these issues do not necessarily disqualify a borrower, they require explanation and documentation. For example, a large deposit may be acceptable if it can be traced to a legitimate business transaction, but it may raise concerns if its source is unclear. Addressing these red flags proactively can strengthen the loan application and improve the likelihood of approval.

The role of compensating factors cannot be overlooked. In cases where income may be borderline or documentation is less than ideal, lenders may consider additional strengths in the borrower's profile. These can include a high credit score, significant cash reserves, a large down payment, or a low debt-to-income ratio. Compensating factors help offset perceived risks and demonstrate the borrower's overall financial stability. For self-employed individuals, leveraging these factors can be a powerful strategy for securing approval.

It is also important to understand that not all lenders evaluate self-employed income in the same way. Different investors have different guidelines, expense ratios, and documentation requirements. This variability means that a borrower who is denied by one lender may be approved by another. Working with a knowledgeable mortgage professional who understands these differences can make a significant impact on the outcome. It allows borrowers to align their financial profile with the most suitable lending program and avoid unnecessary setbacks.

As you begin to navigate the process of qualifying for a mortgage as a self-employed borrower, it is essential to view your income not just as numbers on a page but as a story that needs to be clearly communicated. Every deposit, every expense, and every document contributes to that story. By understanding how lenders interpret this information, you can take control of the narrative and present your financial profile in the strongest possible light. This chapter serves as the foundation for that understanding, setting the stage for the strategies and techniques that will be explored in the chapters ahead.

Real-Life Math Example: Structuring Self-Employed Income for Mortgage Approval

Imagine a self-employed borrower named David, who owns a digital marketing agency. Over the past two years, his business has grown significantly, generating strong monthly revenue. However, like many entrepreneurs, David has used tax deductions to reduce his taxable income, which now shows only $60,000 per year on his tax returns. Based on traditional underwriting guidelines, this income would not be sufficient to qualify for the home he wants to purchase. Fortunately, David decides to explore a bank statement mortgage loan, which allows his income to be evaluated based on his actual cash flow rather than his tax returns.

David provides 12 months of business bank statements showing consistent deposits from client payments. On average, his monthly deposits total $25,000. Over the course of a year, this amounts to $300,000 in gross revenue. The lender reviews these deposits and confirms that they are business-related and recurring. However, the lender must also account for business expenses to determine David's qualifying income. Based on the type of business and industry standards, the lender applies a 50% expense ratio. This means that half of David's revenue is assumed to go toward operating expenses, leaving the remaining 50% as usable income.

Using this calculation, David's monthly qualifying income is determined to be $12,500, which is 50% of his $25,000 in average monthly deposits. Annually, this equates to $150,000 in qualifying income. This is a significant increase compared to the $60,000 reported on his tax returns and provides a much more accurate representation of his financial capacity. With this higher income figure, David is now in a much stronger position to qualify for a mortgage.

Next, the lender evaluates David's debt-to-income ratio. David has monthly obligations that include a car payment of $600, credit card payments totaling $400, and a student loan payment of $300. His total monthly debt is $1,300. The lender calculates his debt-to-income ratio by dividing his total monthly debt by his qualifying income of $12,500, resulting in a ratio of approximately 10.4%. This is well below typical maximum thresholds, indicating that David has ample capacity to take on additional debt in the form of a mortgage.

David is interested in purchasing a home priced at $600,000. He plans to make a 20% down payment, which amounts to $120,000, leaving a loan amount of $480,000. Assuming an interest rate of 7% and a 30-year loan term, his estimated monthly mortgage payment, including principal and interest, is approximately $3,200. When property taxes and insurance are included, the total monthly housing payment rises to around $4,000.

To determine whether David qualifies, the lender adds his proposed housing payment to his existing monthly debt, resulting in total monthly obligations of $5,300. This figure is then divided by his qualifying income of $12,500, producing a total debt-to-income ratio of 42.4%. This falls within acceptable limits for many bank statement loan programs, which often allow ratios up to 50% depending on compensating factors.

In addition to his income and debt profile, David also has strong compensating factors. He has a credit score of 740, which demonstrates a history of responsible credit management. He also maintains cash reserves of $50,000 after his down payment, providing a financial cushion in case of unexpected expenses. These factors further strengthen his application and increase the likelihood of approval.

However, the lender also reviews David's bank statements for any potential red flags. They notice a few large deposits that are higher than his typical monthly revenue. David explains that these were payments from a long-term client who paid for multiple months of services upfront. He provides invoices and contracts to support this explanation, which satisfies the lender's concerns. This highlights the importance of being able to document and explain any irregularities in financial records.

After completing the analysis, the lender determines that David meets all the requirements for the loan. His income, as calculated from his bank statements, supports the proposed mortgage payment, and his overall financial profile demonstrates stability and reliability. Despite having lower taxable income, David is able to qualify for the home he wants by leveraging the flexibility of a bank statement mortgage loan.

This example illustrates how self-employed borrowers can successfully navigate the mortgage process by understanding how their income is evaluated and taking steps to present it effectively. By focusing on cash flow, maintaining consistent deposits, and preparing thorough documentation, borrowers like David can overcome the limitations of traditional underwriting and achieve their homeownership goals.

Chapter 2

Structuring Your Income for Mortgage Approval as a Self-Employed Borrower

One of the most powerful advantages a self-employed borrower has—yet often overlooks—is control. Unlike W-2 employees who receive fixed paychecks, entrepreneurs have the ability to influence how their income appears on paper. This control can either work against them or become their greatest advantage when applying for a mortgage. The difference lies in understanding how lenders interpret financial activity and how to structure that activity in a way that aligns with underwriting guidelines. In this chapter, we will explore how to strategically structure your income, accounts, and financial behavior to maximize your chances of approval using bank statement mortgage loans.

At the core of income structuring is the concept of clarity. Lenders are not just evaluating how much money you make—they are evaluating how clearly your income can be understood and verified. When your financial activity is disorganized, commingled, or inconsistent, it creates uncertainty. Uncertainty increases perceived risk, and perceived risk leads to stricter conditions or denial. On the other hand, when your financial profile is clean, consistent, and easy to interpret, it builds confidence in your ability to repay the loan. Structuring your income begins with eliminating confusion and creating a clear financial narrative.

One of the most important steps in this process is separating personal and business finances. Many self-employed individuals operate with a single account, depositing all income and paying all expenses from the same place. While this may be convenient, it makes it extremely difficult for lenders to distinguish between business revenue, personal transfers, and non-recurring deposits. By maintaining separate accounts for business and personal use, you create a natural structure that simplifies the analysis. Business accounts should reflect revenue and operational expenses, while personal accounts should reflect income available for personal use. This separation alone can significantly strengthen your loan file.

Another critical factor is consistency in deposits. Lenders prefer to see a steady flow of income over time, even if the exact amounts vary. Large fluctuations, gaps in deposits, or irregular patterns can raise concerns about stability. For example, if your business generates significant revenue in some months but little to none in others, it may be perceived as inconsistent, even if the annual income is strong. Structuring your income may involve timing deposits more evenly, maintaining consistent billing cycles, or ensuring that revenue is deposited regularly rather than sporadically. The goal is to create a pattern that demonstrates reliability.

Deposit classification is equally important. Not all deposits are treated the same in underwriting. Business-related deposits are typically included in income calculations, while transfers between accounts, loans, or one-time payments may be excluded. If your bank statements include a mix of deposit types, it is essential to clearly identify and document which deposits represent actual income. This may involve maintaining records such as invoices, contracts, or payment confirmations. By doing so, you help the lender accurately assess your income and avoid unnecessary reductions in qualifying amounts.

Expense management also plays a significant role in structuring income. While it is important to run your business efficiently, excessive or inconsistent expenses can negatively impact how your income is calculated. In bank statement programs, lenders often apply an expense ratio to estimate business costs. However, in some cases, a CPA-prepared profit and loss statement can be used to justify a lower expense ratio. This means that how you track and report your expenses can directly influence your qualifying income. Strategic expense management does not mean inflating profits—it means ensuring that your financial records accurately reflect your business operations.

The timing of your mortgage application is another key consideration. Because bank statement loans typically analyze 12 or 24 months of financial activity, your recent history carries significant weight. If your business has experienced growth, waiting until your higher income levels are reflected in your statements can improve your qualification. Conversely, if you have had a recent decline in revenue, it may be beneficial to stabilize your income before applying. Structuring your income is not just about what you do—it is also about when you do it.

Cash reserves are an often-overlooked component of income structuring. Lenders view reserves as a safety net, indicating that you have the ability to continue making payments even if your income fluctuates. For self-employed borrowers, this is particularly important because income variability is expected. By maintaining strong reserves, you can offset concerns about inconsistent income and strengthen your overall profile. This may involve setting aside a portion of your earnings in savings or investment accounts that can be verified during the loan process.

Another strategy involves reducing unnecessary red flags before applying. This includes minimizing large unexplained deposits, avoiding frequent transfers between accounts, and maintaining consistent account balances. For example, if you regularly move money between personal and business accounts without clear documentation, it can create confusion during underwriting. By simplifying your financial activity and keeping clear records, you reduce the likelihood of questions or delays.

It is also important to consider how your business structure impacts your income presentation. Sole proprietors, partnerships, and corporations each have different financial characteristics. For example, a sole proprietor may have more straightforward income flows, while a corporation may involve distributions, retained earnings, and payroll. Understanding how your specific structure is viewed by lenders allows you to tailor your approach and present your income in the most favorable way.

Working with a knowledgeable mortgage professional can further enhance your income structuring strategy. An experienced loan officer understands the nuances of different lending programs and can guide you in preparing your financial profile. This may include advising on which accounts to use, how to document deposits, and how to address potential issues before they arise. The right guidance can make the difference between a smooth approval process and a challenging one.

Ultimately, structuring your income is about taking control of your financial presentation. As a self-employed borrower, you are not limited by a fixed paycheck—you have the ability to shape how your income is perceived. By creating clear, consistent, and well-documented financial records, you position yourself as a strong and reliable borrower. This chapter provides the foundation for that process, empowering you to approach your mortgage application with confidence and strategy.

Real-Life Math Example: Optimizing Income Structure for Maximum Qualification

Consider a self-employed borrower named Maria, who owns a cleaning services company. Her business generates strong revenue, but her financial records are not structured in a way that maximizes her qualifying income. Maria uses a single bank account for both personal and business transactions, resulting in a mix of deposits that include client payments, personal transfers, and occasional loans from family members. Over the past 12 months, her total deposits average $18,000 per month, but only $14,000 of that represents actual business income.

When Maria first applies for a bank statement loan, the lender reviews her statements and identifies the mixed nature of her deposits. Because some deposits cannot be clearly verified as income, the lender excludes them from the calculation. This reduces her average monthly qualifying deposits to $14,000. The lender then applies a 50% expense ratio, resulting in a qualifying income of $7,000 per month. Based on this income, Maria is limited in the loan amount she can qualify for, and her options are more restricted than she expected.

Recognizing the issue, Maria decides to restructure her financial setup before reapplying. She opens a separate business bank account and begins depositing all client payments into that account exclusively. She also ensures that personal transfers and non-business deposits are kept in her personal account. Over the next 12 months, her business account shows consistent monthly deposits averaging $20,000, all of which are clearly identifiable as income.

When Maria reapplies for a mortgage, the lender reviews her new bank statements. Because the deposits are clean and well-documented, the full $20,000 monthly average is considered. Applying the same 50% expense ratio, her qualifying income increases to $10,000 per month. This represents a significant improvement over her previous qualifying income of $7,000.

Next, the lender evaluates Maria's debt-to-income ratio. She has monthly obligations including a car payment of $500 and credit card payments of $300, totaling $800 in monthly debt. With her new qualifying income of $10,000, her initial debt-to-income ratio is 8%. Maria is interested in purchasing a home with a monthly housing payment of $3,500, including taxes and insurance. Adding this to her existing debt brings her total monthly obligations to $4,300.

Dividing $4,300 by her qualifying income of $10,000 results in a total debt-to-income ratio of 43%. This falls within acceptable limits for many bank statement loan programs. Previously, with a qualifying income of $7,000, the same housing payment would have resulted in a debt-to-income ratio of over 60%, making approval unlikely. By restructuring her income, Maria has transformed her financial profile and significantly improved her chances of approval.

In addition to improving her income structure, Maria also works on reducing red flags. She minimizes transfers between accounts, maintains consistent deposit patterns, and keeps detailed records of all business transactions. She also builds cash reserves of $25,000, which provides additional strength to her application. These changes not only improve her numerical qualifications but also enhance the overall quality of her loan file.

The lender reviews Maria's updated application and finds that her income is stable, her documentation is clear, and her financial profile demonstrates strong repayment ability. As a result, she is approved for the mortgage and able to purchase the home she wants. This example highlights the impact of proper income structuring and the importance of presenting a clear and consistent financial narrative.

Through strategic adjustments to her accounts, deposits, and documentation, Maria was able to increase her qualifying income by over 40% without changing the actual performance of her business. This demonstrates that success in mortgage qualification is not just about how much you earn—it is about how effectively you present and structure that income.

Chapter 3

Reducing Red Flags in Underwriting for Self-Employed Borrowers

For self-employed borrowers, one of the most overlooked yet critical aspects of mortgage approval is not just how much income you show, but how clean, consistent, and understandable your financial profile appears to an underwriter. You may have strong revenue, a profitable business, and years of experience, but if your bank statements raise questions, hesitation is introduced into the decision-making process. In underwriting, hesitation often translates into additional conditions, stricter scrutiny, or even denial. This is why reducing red flags is not optional—it is essential.

A red flag in underwriting is anything that creates uncertainty. Lenders are not just verifying income; they are assessing risk. When something in your financial profile does not clearly make sense, the underwriter must either request more documentation or make a conservative assumption. Both outcomes can work against you. The goal, therefore, is to eliminate as much uncertainty as possible before your file is even reviewed. This means understanding exactly what underwriters look for and proactively structuring your financial activity to align with those expectations.

One of the most common red flags is large, irregular deposits. While high deposits may seem like a positive sign, they can actually create concern if they are not consistent or easily explainable. For example, if your bank statements show typical monthly deposits of $15,000 but suddenly include a $50,000 deposit, the underwriter will want to know where that money came from. If it cannot be verified as recurring business income, it may be excluded from your qualifying income. Worse, it may trigger additional documentation requests that delay your approval. The solution is not to avoid large deposits, but to ensure that they are properly documented with invoices, contracts, or other supporting evidence.

Another major red flag is commingling funds between personal and business accounts. When income and expenses are mixed together, it becomes difficult for underwriters to distinguish between business revenue, personal transfers, and non-income deposits. This confusion can lead to conservative income calculations or the exclusion of certain deposits altogether. For example, if you transfer $5,000 from your business account to your personal account, it may appear as income in one account and a withdrawal in another, creating duplication or misinterpretation. Maintaining separate accounts and minimizing unnecessary transfers helps create clarity and reduces this risk. Declining income trends are also a significant concern. Even if your overall income is strong, a downward trend over the most recent months can signal instability. Lenders are forward-looking—they want to know that you will continue to earn at a level sufficient to repay the loan. If your bank statements show decreasing deposits over time, the underwriter may question the sustainability of your business. To address this, it is important to stabilize your income before applying or be prepared to explain any temporary declines with clear documentation, such as seasonal fluctuations or one-time disruptions.

Frequent non-sufficient funds (NSF) charges or overdrafts can also raise red flags. These indicate poor cash flow management and suggest that you may struggle to meet financial obligations. Even if your income is high, repeated overdrafts can create doubt about your financial discipline. Lenders want to see that you not only earn money but also manage it responsibly. Avoiding overdrafts, maintaining sufficient balances, and demonstrating consistent account management are key to presenting a strong financial profile.

Unexplained transfers between accounts are another area of concern. Moving money frequently between accounts without clear documentation can make it difficult to trace the origin of funds. This is especially problematic when transfers appear as deposits in one account but cannot be linked to a legitimate source. To reduce this red flag, limit transfers to necessary transactions and keep clear records of their purpose. When transfers are unavoidable, ensure that they can be easily explained and documented.

Expense inconsistencies can also impact how your income is evaluated. If your business expenses fluctuate dramatically or appear unusually high, lenders may apply a higher expense ratio, reducing your qualifying income. For example, if your deposits average $20,000 per month but your expenses appear to consume a large portion of that, the lender may assume a lower net income. Keeping consistent and reasonable expense patterns, along with proper documentation, helps ensure that your income is calculated accurately.

Another subtle but important red flag is a lack of documentation. Even if your financial activity is strong, missing or incomplete documentation can delay the process and create doubt. Lenders rely on documentation to verify income, business operations, and financial stability. Providing complete bank statements, business licenses, and supporting documents upfront demonstrates professionalism and preparedness. It also reduces the likelihood of additional conditions and speeds up the approval process.

Credit behavior also plays a role in underwriting perception. While bank statement loans focus on income, your credit profile still matters. Late payments, high credit utilization, or recent derogatory events can raise concerns about your ability to manage debt. Improving your credit profile before applying can serve as a compensating factor and offset minor red flags in your income documentation.

It is important to understand that red flags do not automatically result in denial. However, they do increase scrutiny and may require additional explanations or conditions. The key is to address them proactively rather than reactively. By identifying potential issues in advance and preparing clear explanations and documentation, you can maintain control of the process and avoid unnecessary delays.

Ultimately, reducing red flags is about creating a clean, consistent, and transparent financial profile. As a self-employed borrower, you have the ability to shape how your financial story is presented. By eliminating confusion and demonstrating stability, you build confidence with the lender and position yourself for a successful outcome. This chapter provides the framework for identifying and addressing common red flags, setting the stage for a smoother and more predictable approval process.

Real-Life Math Example: Identifying and Eliminating Red Flags to Improve Loan Approval

Consider a self-employed borrower named Kevin, who owns a landscaping business. Over the past 12 months, Kevin's business has generated strong revenue, with average monthly deposits of $22,000. However, his bank statements contain several red flags that initially prevent him from qualifying for a mortgage. These include large irregular deposits, frequent transfers between accounts, and inconsistent expense patterns.

When Kevin first applies for a bank statement loan, the lender reviews his statements and identifies a $40,000 deposit that does not match his typical monthly income. Kevin explains that this was a one-time payment from a commercial contract, but he does not have documentation to support it. As a result, the lender excludes this deposit from the income calculation. This reduces his average monthly deposits from $22,000 to approximately $19,000.

Next, the lender notices frequent transfers between Kevin's business and personal accounts, totaling about $5,000 per month. Because these transfers cannot be clearly identified as income, they are also excluded. This further reduces his qualifying deposits to $17,000 per month. Applying a 50% expense ratio, the lender calculates Kevin's qualifying income as $8,500 per month. Kevin's monthly debts include a car payment of $700, credit card payments of $500, and a personal loan payment of $300, totaling $1,500. He is seeking a mortgage with a monthly payment of $3,800. Adding this to his existing debt results in total monthly obligations of $5,300. Dividing this by his qualifying income of $8,500 produces a debt-to-income ratio of 62.3%, which exceeds acceptable limits. As a result, Kevin is initially denied.

Determined to improve his chances, Kevin works to eliminate the red flags in his financial profile. First, he begins documenting all large deposits with invoices and contracts. Over the next 12 months, his bank statements show consistent monthly deposits of $23,000, all of which are supported by documentation. This ensures that the full amount can be considered in the income calculation.

Second, Kevin reduces unnecessary transfers between accounts. He maintains a clear separation between business and personal finances, ensuring that all business income is deposited into his business account and only necessary distributions are transferred to his personal account. This eliminates confusion and allows the lender to accurately assess his income.

Third, Kevin stabilizes his expense patterns by maintaining consistent business operations and avoiding large, irregular expenses. He also works with a CPA to prepare a profit and loss statement that supports a lower expense ratio of 40%. This allows the lender to use a more favorable calculation when determining his qualifying income.

With these changes, Kevin reapplies for the mortgage. His average monthly deposits are now $23,000, and with a 40% expense ratio, his qualifying income increases to $13,800 per month. His total monthly obligations, including the proposed mortgage payment, remain at $5,300. Dividing this by his new qualifying income results in a debt-to-income ratio of 38.4%, which falls well within acceptable limits.

In addition to improving his income calculation, Kevin also builds cash reserves of $30,000 and improves his credit score to 720. These compensating factors further strengthen his application and demonstrate financial stability. The lender reviews his updated file and finds that all previous red flags have been addressed. His income is now clear, consistent, and well-documented, and his overall profile meets the requirements for approval.

Kevin is approved for the mortgage and able to purchase the property he wanted. This example illustrates how identifying and eliminating red flags can dramatically improve a borrower's financial profile. By taking control of his financial presentation and addressing issues proactively, Kevin was able to transform a denial into a successful approval.

This case highlights an important lesson for self-employed borrowers: it is not just about how much you earn, but how clearly and consistently that income is presented. Reducing red flags is one of the most effective ways to strengthen your application and achieve your mortgage goals.

Chapter 4

Documentation Strategies for Self-Employed Mortgage Approval

For self-employed borrowers, documentation is not just a requirement—it is the foundation of the entire mortgage approval process. Unlike traditional borrowers who rely on standardized forms like W-2s and pay stubs, entrepreneurs must build a financial story using multiple pieces of evidence. Every bank statement, invoice, license, and financial record becomes part of that story. The strength of your application depends not only on your income but on how clearly and effectively you can document and present it. In this chapter, you will learn how to create a powerful documentation strategy that supports your income, reduces conditions, and positions you for approval.

The first principle of documentation is completeness. Lenders expect a full and uninterrupted record of your financial activity, typically covering 12 or 24 consecutive months. Missing pages, partial statements, or gaps in documentation can immediately raise concerns. Even if your income is strong, incomplete records create uncertainty, and uncertainty leads to delays or denials. It is essential to provide every page of every statement, even if some pages appear irrelevant.

Underwriters are trained to look for consistency across the entire document, and any missing information can disrupt that analysis.

Clarity is equally important. Your documentation should make it easy for an underwriter to understand your income without excessive interpretation. This means organizing your records in a logical and consistent manner. For example, if you are using business bank statements, ensure that all deposits are clearly identifiable as business income. If there are deposits that may not be obvious, such as transfers or one-time payments, provide supporting documentation upfront. This could include invoices, contracts, or written explanations. The goal is to eliminate questions before they arise.

One of the most valuable tools in your documentation strategy is the use of a CPA-prepared profit and loss statement. While bank statements provide a snapshot of your revenue, a profit and loss statement offers a structured view of your business performance. It breaks down income, expenses, and net profit in a way that lenders can easily interpret. In some cases, this document can be used to justify a lower expense ratio, increasing your qualifying income. Working with a CPA to prepare an accurate and professional P&L can significantly strengthen your application. Business licenses and proof of business ownership are also critical components of your documentation. Lenders need to verify that your business is legitimate, active, and stable. This may include a business license, articles of incorporation, or a letter from a CPA confirming your ownership and the nature of your business. These documents provide context for your income and help establish credibility. Without them, even strong financial records may not be sufficient to secure approval.

Another important aspect of documentation is consistency between different records. Your bank statements, P&L, and any other financial documents should align with each other. If your bank statements show $300,000 in annual deposits but your P&L reports significantly lower revenue, the discrepancy must be explained. Inconsistencies create doubt and may lead to conservative assumptions by the lender. Ensuring that all documents tell the same financial story is essential for building confidence in your application.

Letters of explanation are a powerful yet often underutilized tool. These letters allow you to address specific issues in your financial profile, such as large deposits, income fluctuations, or changes in business operations. A well-written letter provides context and helps the underwriter understand the reasoning behind certain transactions. For example, if your income increased significantly due to a new contract, a letter explaining this change, supported by documentation, can turn a potential red flag into a positive factor. Digital organization also plays a role in effective documentation. Submitting your documents in a clear, organized format can streamline the review process and reduce the likelihood of errors. This includes labeling files correctly, grouping related documents together, and ensuring that all pages are legible. A well-organized submission not only makes the underwriter's job easier but also reflects professionalism and attention to detail.

Timing is another critical factor. Because bank statement loans rely on recent financial history, the timing of your documentation can impact your qualification. If your income has improved, waiting until your higher earnings are reflected in your statements can strengthen your application. Conversely, if you have experienced a temporary decline, it may be beneficial to stabilize your income before applying. Strategic timing ensures that your documentation presents your business in the best possible light.

It is also important to anticipate additional documentation requests. Even with a strong initial submission, underwriters may ask for clarification or additional records. Being prepared to respond quickly and thoroughly can prevent delays and keep your application moving forward. This may include having access to invoices, contracts, tax returns, or other supporting documents that can verify your income and business operations. Working with an experienced mortgage professional can greatly enhance your documentation strategy. A knowledgeable loan officer understands what lenders are looking for and can guide you in preparing your documents. They can identify potential issues before submission and help you address them proactively. This collaboration ensures that your application is as strong as possible from the outset.

Ultimately, documentation is about telling a clear and compelling financial story. As a self-employed borrower, you have the opportunity to present your income in a way that reflects the true strength of your business. By focusing on completeness, clarity, consistency, and organization, you can create a documentation strategy that supports your goals and increases your chances of approval. This chapter provides the tools and insights needed to build that strategy and navigate the mortgage process with confidence.

Real-Life Math Example: Using Documentation to Maximize Qualifying Income

Consider a self-employed borrower named Angela, who owns a consulting business. Over the past year, her business has generated strong revenue, with total deposits of $360,000, averaging $30,000 per month. However, her initial documentation is incomplete and disorganized, leading to a lower qualifying income and difficulty in securing approval. When Angela first applies for a bank statement loan, she provides only 10 months of bank statements, missing two months due to oversight. The lender requires a full 12-month history, so the application is delayed until the missing statements are provided. Once submitted, the lender reviews her deposits but identifies several large transactions that cannot be verified as business income. These include transfers from other accounts and a $50,000 deposit from a personal investment. Without supporting documentation, these amounts are excluded from the income calculation.

As a result, Angela's average monthly deposits are reduced from $30,000 to $24,000. The lender applies a standard expense ratio of 50%, resulting in a qualifying income of $12,000 per month. Angela's monthly debts include a car payment of $600 and credit card payments of $400, totaling $1,000. She is seeking a mortgage with a monthly payment of $4,500. Adding this to her existing debt brings her total monthly obligations to $5,500.

Dividing $5,500 by her qualifying income of $12,000 results in a debt-to-income ratio of 45.8%, which is near the upper limit for many programs. While this may still be acceptable, the presence of documentation issues and unverified deposits weakens her application and leads to additional conditions.

Angela decides to improve her documentation strategy before proceeding. She works with her CPA to prepare a detailed profit and loss statement that accurately reflects her business income and expenses. The P&L shows that her actual expense ratio is closer to 35%, significantly lower than the standard 50% used by the lender. She also gathers supporting documents for all large deposits, including invoices, contracts, and bank transfer records.

When Angela resubmits her application, the lender reviews her updated documentation. With all deposits now verified as business income, her average monthly deposits are restored to $30,000. Using the CPA-prepared P&L, the lender applies a 35% expense ratio, resulting in a qualifying income of $19,500 per month.

With this higher income, Angela's total monthly obligations of $5,500 result in a debt-to-income ratio of 28.2%, well within acceptable limits. The improved documentation not only increases her qualifying income but also strengthens her overall profile by eliminating uncertainty and demonstrating financial stability.

Additionally, Angela provides a letter of explanation for her investment deposit, clarifying that it is not part of her business income. This transparency further enhances the credibility of her application. She also organizes her documents in a clear and professional format, making it easy for the underwriter to review and verify her information.

The lender approves Angela's loan, and she is able to secure the mortgage with favorable terms. This example demonstrates the impact of a strong documentation strategy on mortgage approval. By providing complete, clear, and consistent records, Angela was able to increase her qualifying income by over 60% and significantly improve her debt-to-income ratio.

This case highlights a critical lesson for self-employed borrowers: documentation is not just a requirement—it is an opportunity. By taking control of how your financial information is presented, you can maximize your qualifying income and position yourself for success in the mortgage process.

Chapter 5

Bank Statement Mortgage Loans for Primary Residences

Purchasing or refinancing a primary residence is one of the most important financial decisions a self-employed borrower can make, yet it is often the most challenging when traditional income documentation does not reflect true earning power. For entrepreneurs, business owners, and independent contractors, qualifying for a home using tax returns alone can feel limiting, especially when legitimate deductions reduce reported income. Bank statement mortgage loans provide a powerful alternative by allowing borrowers to qualify based on actual cash flow rather than taxable income. When applied to primary residences, these programs open the door to homeownership while still maintaining structured guidelines that lenders use to manage risk.

Primary residence financing is viewed differently by lenders compared to investment properties or second homes. Because a primary residence is where the borrower lives, it is generally considered lower risk. Borrowers are more likely to prioritize payments on their primary home, which allows lenders to offer more favorable terms. However, this also means that lenders apply stricter guidelines in certain areas to ensure long-term stability. For self-employed borrowers, understanding these guidelines is essential to structuring a successful loan application.

One of the most important factors in primary residence bank statement loans is occupancy. The borrower must intend to live in the property as their main home. This affects not only the loan terms but also the documentation required. Lenders may request proof of occupancy, such as utility bills, driver's license updates, or a letter of intent. Misrepresenting occupancy can lead to serious consequences, including loan denial or future legal issues. Therefore, it is critical to be accurate and transparent about how the property will be used.

Loan-to-value ratio, or LTV, is another key component. LTV represents the percentage of the property's value that is financed by the loan. For primary residences, bank statement programs often allow higher LTVs compared to investment properties, sometimes reaching up to 90% depending on credit score and other factors. A higher LTV means a lower down payment, making homeownership more accessible. However, higher LTVs may also come with stricter requirements, such as higher credit scores or additional reserves. Understanding how LTV impacts your loan structure allows you to balance affordability with approval strength. Reserves are particularly important for self-employed borrowers purchasing a primary residence. Reserves refer to the amount of liquid assets you have available after closing, typically measured in months of mortgage payments. For example, if your monthly housing payment is $4,000 and the lender requires six months of reserves, you would need $24,000 in accessible funds. Reserves provide a safety net for lenders, demonstrating that you can continue making payments even if your income fluctuates. Strong reserves can also serve as a compensating factor, helping offset other areas of concern.

Debt-to-income ratio remains a central metric in determining loan eligibility. For bank statement loans, this ratio is calculated using qualifying income derived from deposits rather than tax returns. For primary residences, lenders may allow higher debt-to-income ratios compared to other property types, sometimes up to 50%, depending on the overall strength of the borrower's profile. However, lower ratios are always more favorable and can lead to better loan terms. Structuring your income and managing your debts effectively can significantly impact this calculation.

Interest rates for bank statement loans on primary residences are typically higher than those for traditional loans, reflecting the additional risk associated with alternative documentation. However, these rates can vary widely based on credit score, LTV, reserves, and overall borrower strength. Improving these factors before applying can help secure more favorable terms. It is important to view the interest rate not just as a cost but as part of a broader strategy to achieve homeownership when traditional options are not available.

Another important consideration is property type. While primary residences generally include single-family homes, condos, and townhouses, certain property characteristics may impact eligibility. For example, unique or non-standard properties may require additional appraisal considerations. Ensuring that the property meets lender guidelines is an essential step in the process. Working with experienced professionals can help identify potential issues early and avoid delays.

Refinancing a primary residence using bank statement income follows similar principles but with additional opportunities. Cash-out refinancing allows borrowers to access equity in their home, which can be used for business investment, debt consolidation, or other financial goals. Rate-and-term refinancing can help reduce monthly payments or secure more favorable loan terms. For self-employed borrowers, these options provide flexibility and access to capital that may not be available through traditional lending channels. One of the most powerful aspects of bank statement loans for primary residences is the ability to align your mortgage with your actual financial reality. Instead of being constrained by tax return figures, you can leverage your true income to qualify for the home you want. This shift in perspective transforms the mortgage process from a limitation into an opportunity. By understanding the guidelines and structuring your financial profile accordingly, you can navigate the process with confidence and clarity.

Ultimately, purchasing or refinancing a primary residence as a self-employed borrower is about more than just meeting requirements—it is about presenting a complete and compelling financial picture. Every element, from your bank statements to your reserves, contributes to that picture. By mastering these components, you position yourself not only for approval but for long-term success as a homeowner. This chapter provides the framework for understanding how bank statement loans apply to primary residences and how to use them effectively to achieve your goals.

Real-Life Math Example: Qualifying for a Primary Residence Using Bank Statement Income

Consider a self-employed borrower named Daniel, who owns a construction business. Daniel has been renting for several years and now wants to purchase a primary residence for his family. His business generates strong revenue, but his tax returns show only $80,000 in annual income due to significant deductions. Based on traditional lending guidelines, this income would limit his purchasing power. However, Daniel decides to pursue a bank statement mortgage loan to qualify based on his actual cash flow.

Daniel provides 12 months of business bank statements showing total deposits of $360,000, averaging $30,000 per month. The lender reviews these deposits and confirms that they are consistent and primarily derived from business operations. To determine qualifying income, the lender applies a 50% expense ratio, resulting in a monthly income of $15,000. Annually, this equates to $180,000 in qualifying income, more than double what is reflected on his tax returns.

Daniel's existing monthly debts include a truck payment of $800, credit card payments of $500, and a small business loan payment of $700, totaling $2,000. With a qualifying income of $15,000, his initial debt-to-income ratio is 13.3%. This provides a strong foundation for adding a mortgage payment.

Daniel is interested in purchasing a home priced at $700,000. He plans to make a 15% down payment, which amounts to $105,000, resulting in a loan amount of $595,000. Assuming an interest rate of 7.25% and a 30-year term, his estimated monthly principal and interest payment is approximately $4,060. Adding property taxes and insurance brings his total monthly housing payment to $4,800.

To calculate his total debt-to-income ratio, the lender adds his housing payment to his existing debt, resulting in total monthly obligations of $6,800. Dividing this by his qualifying income of $15,000 produces a ratio of 45.3%, which falls within acceptable limits for many bank statement loan programs.

Next, the lender evaluates Daniel's loan-to-value ratio. With a purchase price of $700,000 and a loan amount of $595,000, his LTV is approximately 85%. This is within the allowable range for primary residence bank statement loans, although it may require a higher credit score or additional reserves.

Daniel has a credit score of 720 and maintains cash reserves of $40,000 after his down payment. With a monthly housing payment of $4,800, his reserves cover approximately 8.3 months of payments, exceeding the typical requirement of six months. These strong compensating factors further support his application.

The lender reviews Daniel's bank statements for any red flags and finds consistent deposits with no significant irregularities. His documentation is complete, and his financial profile demonstrates stability and reliability. Based on this analysis, the lender approves his loan. This example illustrates how bank statement income can significantly increase purchasing power for self-employed borrowers. By using his actual cash flow rather than his tax returns, Daniel was able to qualify for a home that aligns with his true financial capacity. His strong income, combined with manageable debt, adequate reserves, and a reasonable LTV, created a well-balanced application that met lender requirements.

Through proper structuring and understanding of the process, Daniel transformed his financial profile into a powerful tool for achieving homeownership. This case highlights the importance of leveraging bank statement loans effectively and demonstrates how self-employed borrowers can successfully navigate the mortgage process for primary residences.

Chapter 6

Bank Statement Mortgage Loans for Investment Properties

For self-employed borrowers, the ability to finance investment properties is one of the most powerful ways to build long-term wealth. Real estate investing offers the potential for cash flow, appreciation, tax advantages, and portfolio growth, but accessing financing can be challenging when traditional income documentation does not fully reflect earning capacity. Bank statement mortgage loans provide a flexible solution by allowing investors to qualify based on actual cash flow rather than tax returns. When applied strategically, these loans can serve as a foundation for scaling a real estate portfolio and creating consistent income streams.

Investment properties are evaluated differently from primary residences because they are considered higher risk. Lenders understand that borrowers are more likely to prioritize payments on their primary home, so they apply stricter guidelines to investment loans. This includes lower maximum loan-to-value ratios, higher reserve requirements, and more conservative debt-to-income limits. However, for self-employed borrowers with strong cash flow, bank statement loans still offer a viable and effective path to financing these properties.

One of the most important concepts in investment property financing is the relationship between personal income and property income. While bank statement loans focus on the borrower's income, many lenders also consider the projected rental income of the property. This is where strategies such as combining bank statement income with debt service coverage ratio (DSCR) analysis can become highly effective. DSCR measures the property's ability to generate enough income to cover its debt obligations. When both borrower income and property income are strong, the overall risk profile improves, increasing the likelihood of approval.

Loan-to-value ratios for investment properties are typically lower than those for primary residences, often ranging from 70% to 80% depending on the borrower's profile. This means that investors must provide a larger down payment, which can impact initial capital requirements. However, a lower LTV also reduces risk for the lender and can lead to better loan terms. For self-employed investors, balancing down payment size with available liquidity is a key part of structuring a successful deal.

Reserves play an even more significant role in investment property loans. Lenders want to ensure that borrowers have sufficient funds to cover both personal obligations and property-related expenses in case of vacancies or unexpected costs. Reserve requirements may range from six to twelve months of mortgage payments, and in some cases, additional reserves may be required for multiple properties. Strong reserves not only satisfy lender requirements but also provide a financial cushion that supports long-term investment success.

Debt-to-income ratio remains an important factor, but it is often evaluated more conservatively for investment properties. Lenders may allow ratios up to 45% or 50% depending on compensating factors, but lower ratios are generally preferred. For self-employed borrowers, maximizing qualifying income through proper structuring of bank statements can significantly improve this ratio. At the same time, managing existing debts and avoiding unnecessary liabilities can further strengthen the application.

Another key consideration is the type of property being financed. Single-family rental properties, multi-unit properties, and short-term rental properties each have unique characteristics that influence underwriting. For example, short-term rentals such as vacation properties may require additional documentation to verify income potential, while multi-unit properties may involve more complex cash flow analysis. Understanding how different property types are evaluated allows investors to choose opportunities that align with their financing strategy.

Scaling a portfolio using bank statement loans requires careful planning and consistency. Each additional property adds to the borrower's overall financial profile, increasing both income and obligations. Lenders will evaluate the entire portfolio when considering new loans, so maintaining strong performance across all properties is essential. This includes consistent rental income, timely payments, and adequate reserves. By building a track record of successful investments, self-employed borrowers can position themselves for continued growth.

Refinancing plays a critical role in investment property strategy. Cash-out refinancing allows investors to access equity from existing properties, which can then be used to fund additional purchases. This creates a cycle of reinvestment that accelerates portfolio expansion. Bank statement loans can be used for refinancing as well, providing flexibility for self-employed borrowers who may not qualify under traditional guidelines. Understanding when and how to refinance is key to maximizing returns and maintaining liquidity.

Risk management is another important aspect of investment property financing. While the potential for profit is significant, so are the risks associated with vacancies, market fluctuations, and unexpected expenses. Lenders account for these risks through stricter guidelines, but investors must also take responsibility for managing them. This includes maintaining reserves, diversifying properties, and ensuring that each investment is financially viable. A disciplined approach to risk management not only supports loan approval but also contributes to long-term success.

Ultimately, bank statement mortgage loans for investment properties provide a pathway for self-employed borrowers to leverage their income and build wealth through real estate. By understanding the unique requirements and structuring deals effectively, investors can overcome the limitations of traditional financing and create opportunities for growth. This chapter provides the framework for navigating investment property loans, empowering you to take control of your financial future and expand your real estate portfolio with confidence.

Real-Life Math Example: Scaling an Investment Property Portfolio Using Bank Statement Income

Consider a self-employed borrower named Lisa, who owns a marketing agency and is looking to invest in rental properties.

Lisa's business generates strong revenue, with average monthly deposits of $28,000, totaling $336,000 annually. Using a bank statement loan, the lender applies a 50% expense ratio, resulting in a qualifying income of $14,000 per month. Lisa currently owns one rental property with a monthly mortgage payment of $2,000 and rental income of $2,500, producing a positive cash flow of $500. Her personal monthly debts include a car payment of $600 and credit card payments of $400, totaling $1,000. Her total existing obligations are $3,000 per month.

Lisa wants to purchase a second investment property priced at $400,000. The lender requires a 25% down payment, which amounts to $100,000, resulting in a loan amount of $300,000. At an interest rate of 7.5% over 30 years, the monthly principal and interest payment is approximately $2,100. Including taxes and insurance, the total monthly housing cost is $2,600.

The property is expected to generate rental income of $3,200 per month. The lender evaluates the debt service coverage ratio by dividing the rental income by the property's total monthly payment. In this case, the DSCR is approximately 1.23, indicating that the property generates more income than required to cover its debt. This positive cash flow strengthens Lisa's application.

Next, the lender calculates Lisa's total monthly obligations. Her existing obligations of $3,000 are combined with the new property's payment of $2,600, resulting in total obligations of $5,600. Dividing this by her qualifying income of $14,000 produces a debt-to-income ratio of 40%, which falls within acceptable limits.

The lender also considers the rental income from both properties. Her first property generates $2,500 per month, and the new property is expected to generate $3,200, resulting in total rental income of $5,700. This additional income further supports her ability to manage multiple properties.

Lisa has cash reserves of $60,000 after her down payment, which covers more than 10 months of combined mortgage payments across both properties. This exceeds the lender's reserve requirements and demonstrates strong financial stability. She also has a credit score of 730, which contributes to favorable loan terms.

Based on this analysis, the lender approves Lisa's loan for the second investment property. After the purchase, her portfolio includes two properties with combined positive cash flow and strong income support. Encouraged by this success, Lisa plans to continue expanding her portfolio.

Over time, Lisa uses cash-out refinancing to access equity from her properties. For example, if her first property increases in value to $350,000 and she refinances at 75% LTV, she can access approximately $262,500 in loan proceeds. After paying off the existing loan balance of $250,000, she receives $12,500 in cash, which can be used toward her next investment.

By repeating this process and leveraging her bank statement income, Lisa gradually builds a portfolio of multiple properties. Each property contributes to her overall income and strengthens her financial position. Her strategy demonstrates how self-employed borrowers can use bank statement loans not just to qualify for a single property, but to scale a real estate portfolio over time.

This example highlights the power of combining income structuring, property cash flow analysis, and strategic financing. By understanding how lenders evaluate investment properties and aligning her financial profile accordingly, Lisa is able to achieve her investment goals and create long-term wealth through real estate.

Chapter 7

Jumbo Bank Statement Mortgage Loans

Jumbo mortgage loans represent a unique and powerful opportunity for self-employed borrowers who are looking to finance high-value properties that exceed conventional loan limits. These loans are designed for borrowers purchasing or refinancing properties in higher price ranges, often in competitive or luxury markets. For entrepreneurs and business owners, jumbo bank statement loans offer the ability to qualify based on real cash flow rather than tax returns, making them especially valuable for individuals whose income is strong but not fully reflected on paper. However, with greater opportunity comes greater scrutiny, and understanding how jumbo loans are structured is essential to achieving approval.

A jumbo loan is typically defined as any mortgage that exceeds the conforming loan limits set by government-sponsored entities. Because these loans are not backed by those entities, lenders take on more risk and therefore apply stricter underwriting guidelines. For self-employed borrowers, this means that while bank statement programs provide flexibility in income documentation, other aspects of the loan—such as credit, reserves, and overall financial strength—must be exceptionally solid. Jumbo loans are not just about qualifying; they are about demonstrating a high level of financial stability and responsibility.

One of the most important factors in jumbo bank statement loans is income strength. While standard bank statement loans may allow for moderate variability in income, jumbo loans require a higher level of consistency and reliability. Lenders want to see strong, stable deposits over a 12- or 24-month period, with minimal fluctuations and clear documentation. Because the loan amounts are larger, the margin for error is smaller. Any inconsistencies in income can have a greater impact on the overall risk profile, making it essential to present a clean and well-structured financial history.

Credit score requirements are also more stringent for jumbo loans. While standard programs may allow credit scores in the mid-600s, jumbo loans often require scores of 700 or higher, with the best terms reserved for borrowers with scores above 720 or 740. A strong credit profile demonstrates a history of responsible financial behavior and reduces perceived risk for the lender. For self-employed borrowers, maintaining excellent credit is one of the most effective ways to strengthen a jumbo loan application.

Loan-to-value ratios for jumbo bank statement loans are typically lower than those for smaller loans. While standard programs may allow LTVs up to 90% for primary residences, jumbo loans often cap LTV at 70% to 80%, depending on the borrower's profile. This means that larger down payments are required, which can significantly impact the initial investment. However, a lower LTV also reduces risk and can lead to more favorable loan terms. For high-value properties, this balance between down payment and loan amount is a critical consideration.

Reserves play a central role in jumbo loan approval. Because of the higher loan amounts, lenders require borrowers to have substantial liquid assets available after closing. Reserve requirements may range from 12 to 24 months of mortgage payments, and in some cases, even higher for multiple properties or complex financial profiles. These reserves provide a safety net and demonstrate that the borrower can sustain payments even in the face of income fluctuations. For self-employed individuals, strong reserves can be a decisive factor in securing approval.

Debt-to-income ratio remains an important metric, but it is often evaluated more conservatively in jumbo loans. While some programs may allow ratios up to 45%, many lenders prefer lower ratios, especially for higher loan amounts. This means that managing existing debts and maximizing qualifying income are essential. For self-employed borrowers, this involves careful structuring of bank statements, minimizing unnecessary liabilities, and ensuring that income calculations are as favorable as possible.

Another key consideration is the property itself. Jumbo loans are often used to finance luxury homes, which may have unique features or higher maintenance costs. Lenders evaluate not only the borrower but also the property's marketability and value. Appraisals for jumbo properties can be more complex, requiring additional analysis and sometimes multiple appraisals. Ensuring that the property meets lender guidelines and is supported by a strong appraisal is an important part of the process.

Interest rates for jumbo bank statement loans are typically higher than those for conforming loans, reflecting the increased risk. However, these rates can vary significantly based on the borrower's profile. Strong credit, low LTV, high reserves, and stable income can all contribute to more favorable terms. For self-employed borrowers, improving these factors before applying can make a substantial difference in the cost of the loan.

Strategic planning is essential when pursuing a jumbo loan. Because of the complexity and higher requirements, preparation is key. This includes organizing financial documents, stabilizing income, building reserves, and addressing any potential red flags. Working with experienced professionals who understand jumbo lending can also provide valuable guidance and help navigate the process more effectively.

Ultimately, jumbo bank statement mortgage loans provide an opportunity for self-employed borrowers to access high-value properties that might otherwise be out of reach. By understanding the unique requirements and structuring your financial profile accordingly, you can position yourself for success. This chapter provides the insights needed to navigate jumbo lending and leverage your income to achieve your real estate goals.

Real-Life Math Example: Qualifying for a Jumbo Property Using Bank Statement Income

Consider a self-employed borrower named Robert, who owns a successful technology consulting firm. Robert is interested in purchasing a luxury home priced at $1,500,000. His tax returns show an annual income of $120,000 due to business deductions, but his actual cash flow is significantly higher. To qualify for the loan, he decides to use a jumbo bank statement mortgage program. Robert provides 24 months of business bank statements showing total deposits of $1,200,000, averaging $50,000 per month. The lender reviews these deposits and confirms that they are consistent and derived from business operations. To calculate qualifying income, the lender applies a 50% expense ratio, resulting in a monthly income of $25,000, or $300,000 annually.

Robert plans to make a 25% down payment, which amounts to $375,000, resulting in a loan amount of $1,125,000. Assuming an interest rate of 7% and a 30-year term, his monthly principal and interest payment is approximately $7,500. Including taxes and insurance, the total monthly housing payment is estimated at $9,000.

Robert's existing monthly debts include a car payment of $1,000 and credit card payments of $500, totaling $1,500. Adding his housing payment results in total monthly obligations of $10,500. Dividing this by his qualifying income of $25,000 produces a debt-to-income ratio of 42%, which is within acceptable limits for many jumbo loan programs.

Next, the lender evaluates Robert's loan-to-value ratio. With a purchase price of $1,500,000 and a loan amount of $1,125,000, his LTV is 75%, which falls within typical jumbo guidelines. His credit score is 760, which qualifies him for more favorable terms and demonstrates strong financial responsibility.

The lender also reviews Robert's reserves. After his down payment, he has $150,000 in liquid assets. With a monthly housing payment of $9,000, this provides approximately 16.7 months of reserves, exceeding the lender's requirement of 12 months. These strong reserves further enhance his application.

During the review process, the lender identifies a few large deposits that exceed Robert's typical monthly revenue. Robert provides documentation showing that these deposits are from long-term contracts paid in advance. This explanation satisfies the lender and allows the deposits to be included in the income calculation.

Based on this analysis, Robert meets all the requirements for the jumbo loan. His strong income, low LTV, excellent credit, and substantial reserves create a well-balanced and low-risk profile. The lender approves his loan, and he is able to purchase the luxury home.

This example demonstrates how self-employed borrowers can leverage bank statement income to qualify for high-value properties. By focusing on cash flow, maintaining strong financial metrics, and preparing thorough documentation, borrowers like Robert can successfully navigate the complexities of jumbo lending and achieve their real estate goals.

Chapter 8

Bank Statement Mortgage Loan Refinancing & Cash-Out Strategies

For self-employed borrowers, refinancing is not just a way to adjust a mortgage—it is a strategic financial tool that can unlock liquidity, reduce risk, and accelerate wealth-building. Unlike traditional borrowers who rely on fixed income documentation, entrepreneurs often face limitations when trying to refinance using tax returns. Bank statement mortgage loans remove this barrier by allowing refinancing based on actual cash flow, providing access to opportunities that would otherwise remain out of reach. Whether the goal is to lower monthly payments, access equity, or restructure debt, understanding how to use refinancing strategically is essential.

Refinancing generally falls into two primary categories: rate-and-term refinancing and cash-out refinancing. A rate-and-term refinance focuses on improving the existing loan by lowering the interest rate, extending or shortening the loan term, or switching from an adjustable to a fixed rate. For self-employed borrowers, this can provide stability and reduce monthly obligations, especially if their financial situation has improved since the original loan was obtained. Bank statement loans make this possible even when tax returns do not reflect sufficient income.

Cash-out refinancing, on the other hand, allows borrowers to access the equity they have built in their property. This is particularly powerful for entrepreneurs, as it converts illiquid equity into usable capital. The funds can be used for a wide range of purposes, including business expansion, real estate investment, debt consolidation, or even creating additional income streams. For self-employed individuals, this flexibility can be transformative, turning home equity into a tool for growth rather than a static asset.

One of the most important concepts in refinancing is equity. Equity represents the difference between the property's value and the outstanding loan balance. As property values increase and loan balances decrease, equity grows. Lenders use loan-to-value ratios to determine how much equity can be accessed. For example, if a lender allows a maximum LTV of 80%, a borrower with a property valued at $500,000 can have a loan balance of up to $400,000. If the current loan balance is $300,000, the borrower may be able to access up to $100,000 in cash through refinancing.

For bank statement cash-out refinances, LTV limits are often slightly lower than for purchase loans, typically ranging from 70% to 80% depending on the borrower's profile. This ensures that sufficient equity remains in the property after the refinance. While this may limit the amount of cash that can be accessed, it also reduces risk and helps maintain long-term financial stability. Understanding how LTV impacts your available equity is a key part of planning a successful refinance.

Debt-to-income ratio continues to play a central role in refinancing decisions. When accessing cash-out funds, borrowers often increase their loan balance and, consequently, their monthly payment. Lenders must ensure that the borrower's income can support this higher obligation. For self-employed borrowers, this means that qualifying income derived from bank statements must be sufficient not only for the existing loan but also for the new, larger payment. Structuring income effectively before refinancing can significantly improve the outcome.

Another critical factor is the purpose of the cash-out funds. While lenders do not always restrict how the funds are used, the borrower's financial strategy should be carefully considered. Using cash-out funds to pay off high-interest debt can improve overall cash flow and reduce financial stress. Investing in additional income-producing assets, such as rental properties or business expansion, can create new revenue streams. However, using funds for non-productive purposes may increase financial risk without providing long-term benefits. Strategic use of equity is essential for maximizing the advantages of refinancing.

Timing is also a key consideration. Market conditions, interest rates, and property values all influence the effectiveness of a refinance. For example, refinancing when property values are high can increase available equity, while refinancing when interest rates are lower can reduce monthly payments. For self-employed borrowers, timing also involves ensuring that bank statements reflect strong and consistent income. Waiting until your financial profile is at its strongest can lead to better terms and higher approval chances.

Reserves remain an important requirement in refinancing, especially for cash-out transactions. Lenders want to ensure that borrowers retain sufficient liquidity after accessing equity. This means that even after receiving cash-out funds, borrowers may be required to maintain a certain level of reserves. Planning for this requirement is essential to avoid unexpected challenges during the approval process.

Another important aspect of refinancing is the impact on long-term financial goals. While accessing equity can provide immediate benefits, it also increases the loan balance and potentially extends the repayment period. Borrowers must consider how this aligns with their overall strategy, whether it is building wealth, reducing debt, or improving cash flow. A well-planned refinance should support both short-term needs and long-term objectives.

Working with experienced professionals is particularly valuable in refinancing scenarios. The complexity of bank statement loans, combined with the strategic nature of cash-out decisions, requires careful planning and execution. A knowledgeable mortgage professional can help evaluate options, structure the loan, and ensure that all requirements are met. This guidance can make the difference between a successful refinance and a missed opportunity.

Ultimately, refinancing with bank statement mortgage loans provides self-employed borrowers with a powerful tool for financial flexibility. By understanding the mechanics of rate-and-term and cash-out refinancing, and by aligning these strategies with your financial goals, you can unlock the full potential of your real estate assets. This chapter provides the framework for using refinancing effectively, empowering you to make informed decisions and take control of your financial future.

Real-Life Math Example: Using Cash-Out Refinancing to Build Wealth

Consider a self-employed borrower named James, who owns a home currently valued at $600,000. His existing mortgage balance is $350,000, and his monthly payment is $2,500. Over the years, his property has appreciated in value, and he has built significant equity. James wants to use this equity to invest in additional real estate, but his tax returns show limited income due to business deductions. He decides to pursue a bank statement cash-out refinance.

James provides 12 months of bank statements showing average monthly deposits of $24,000. The lender applies a 50% expense ratio, resulting in a qualifying income of $12,000 per month. His existing debts include a car payment of $600 and credit card payments of $400, totaling $1,000.

The lender allows a maximum LTV of 80% for the cash-out refinance. Based on the property value of $600,000, the maximum loan amount is $480,000. Subtracting the existing loan balance of $350,000, James can access up to $130,000 in cash. He decides to proceed with a new loan amount of $480,000.

At an interest rate of 7.25% over 30 years, the new monthly principal and interest payment is approximately $3,275.

Including taxes and insurance, the total monthly payment is $3,800. Adding his existing debt of $1,000 results in total monthly obligations of $4,800.

Dividing $4,800 by his qualifying income of $12,000 produces a debt-to-income ratio of 40%, which falls within acceptable limits. The lender also requires six months of reserves, which for a $3,800 monthly payment amounts to $22,800. After the refinance, James retains $30,000 in savings, meeting this requirement.

With $130,000 in cash-out funds, James decides to purchase an investment property priced at $400,000, using $100,000 as a down payment and reserving the remaining $30,000 for closing costs and additional reserves. The new property generates rental income of $3,000 per month, with a mortgage payment of $2,400, resulting in positive cash flow of $600.

By leveraging his home equity, James has effectively turned a static asset into an income-producing investment. His overall financial position improves as he adds a new revenue stream while maintaining manageable debt levels. Over time, the appreciation of both properties and the additional rental income contribute to his long-term wealth.

This example demonstrates how cash-out refinancing can be used strategically to create opportunities for growth. By understanding how to calculate equity, structure income, and manage debt, self-employed borrowers can use bank statement loans to access capital and build a stronger financial future.

Chapter 9

Bank Statement Mortgage Loans with Low Credit or Financial Challenges

For many self-employed borrowers, the challenge of qualifying for a mortgage extends beyond income documentation. While bank statement loans solve the issue of reduced taxable income, credit history and past financial events can still create significant barriers. Life happens—business downturns, unexpected expenses, market shifts, or personal circumstances can impact credit. The key is understanding that imperfect credit does not automatically disqualify you. In fact, bank statement mortgage programs are specifically designed to provide flexibility for borrowers with non-traditional profiles, including those with lower credit scores or past financial challenges. The goal is not perfection, but the ability to demonstrate recovery, stability, and responsibility moving forward.

Credit is a reflection of past behavior, but underwriting is focused on future risk. Lenders want to know whether you are likely to repay the loan based on your current financial situation. This means that even if you have experienced credit issues in the past, what matters most is how you have managed your finances recently. Bank statement loans often allow lower credit scores than traditional programs, sometimes starting in the mid-600s or even lower depending on compensating factors. However, lower credit scores typically come with stricter requirements, such as higher down payments, lower loan-to-value ratios, and increased reserve requirements.

One of the most important concepts in this space is credit event seasoning. Major credit events such as bankruptcies, foreclosures, or short sales require a certain amount of time to pass before a borrower can qualify for a new mortgage. This period allows lenders to assess whether the borrower has re-established financial stability. For example, a borrower who experienced a foreclosure three years ago but has maintained perfect payment history since then may be viewed more favorably than someone with recent late payments. Understanding seasoning requirements and planning accordingly is essential for timing your application.

Compensating factors become especially important when credit is less than ideal. These factors help offset perceived risk and demonstrate overall financial strength. Examples include strong income, large down payments, significant cash reserves, low debt-to-income ratios, and stable business operations. For self-employed borrowers, bank statement income can serve as a powerful compensating factor, particularly when it shows consistent and substantial cash flow. By strengthening other areas of your financial profile, you can balance out credit challenges and improve your chances of approval.

Loan-to-value ratios are typically more conservative for borrowers with lower credit scores. While higher-credit borrowers may qualify for LTVs up to 85% or 90%, those with credit challenges may be limited to 70% or 75%. This means a larger down payment is required, which reduces risk for the lender and demonstrates commitment from the borrower. Although this may increase the upfront investment, it can also lead to better loan terms and a stronger overall application.

Interest rates are another factor influenced by credit. Borrowers with lower credit scores generally receive higher interest rates to compensate for increased risk. However, these rates are not permanent. By improving credit over time, borrowers may have the opportunity to refinance into more favorable terms in the future. Viewing the initial loan as a stepping stone rather than a final destination can help frame the process in a more strategic way.

Another important aspect is addressing recent credit behavior. Even if you have a history of credit challenges, demonstrating positive financial habits in the present can significantly improve your profile. This includes making all payments on time, reducing credit card balances, and avoiding new debt before applying for a mortgage. Lenders place a strong emphasis on recent activity, so focusing on the last 12 to 24 months can have a meaningful impact.

Documentation and explanation are critical when dealing with credit challenges. Lenders may require letters of explanation for past events, detailing what happened and how the situation has been resolved. A clear and honest explanation, supported by documentation, can help underwriters understand the context and reduce concerns. For example, a temporary business downturn that led to late payments may be viewed differently if it is followed by a period of strong recovery and consistent performance.

It is also important to manage expectations. While bank statement loans provide flexibility, they are not designed to eliminate all requirements. Borrowers with credit challenges may need to accept certain trade-offs, such as higher rates or lower LTVs. However, these trade-offs can be part of a broader strategy to achieve homeownership or investment goals. Once the loan is secured, borrowers can work toward improving their financial profile and refinancing in the future.

Working with the right lender and mortgage professional is particularly important in these situations. Not all lenders have the same guidelines or risk tolerance, and some are more experienced in working with borrowers who have credit challenges. Finding a lender that understands your situation and offers appropriate programs can make a significant difference in the outcome.

Ultimately, bank statement mortgage loans provide a pathway for self-employed borrowers to overcome credit challenges and move forward. By focusing on current financial strength, leveraging compensating factors, and presenting a clear and well-documented application, you can demonstrate your ability to repay the loan and achieve your goals. This chapter provides the framework for navigating credit challenges and turning potential obstacles into opportunities.

Real-Life Math Example: Qualifying with Lower Credit Using Compensating Factors

Consider a self-employed borrower named Anthony, who owns a trucking business. Anthony experienced financial difficulties two years ago due to a temporary downturn in his industry, which resulted in late payments and a drop in his credit score to 640. Since then, he has rebuilt his business and now generates strong revenue, but his credit history still presents a challenge when applying for a mortgage.

Anthony provides 12 months of bank statements showing average monthly deposits of $26,000, totaling $312,000 annually. The lender applies a 50% expense ratio, resulting in a qualifying income of $13,000 per month. Despite his lower credit score, this strong income serves as a key compensating factor.

Anthony's existing monthly debts include a truck payment of $900, credit card payments of $600, and a personal loan payment of $500, totaling $2,000. With a qualifying income of $13,000, his initial debt-to-income ratio is approximately 15.4%. This low ratio demonstrates strong capacity to take on additional debt.

Anthony is interested in purchasing a home priced at $400,000. Due to his credit score, the lender requires a 25% down payment, which amounts to $100,000, resulting in a loan amount of $300,000. At an interest rate of 7.75% over 30 years, his monthly principal and interest payment is approximately $2,150. Including taxes and insurance, the total monthly housing payment is $2,700.

Adding his housing payment to his existing debt results in total monthly obligations of $4,700. Dividing this by his qualifying income of $13,000 produces a debt-to-income ratio of 36.1%, which falls within acceptable limits. His strong income and manageable debt help offset his lower credit score. The lender also evaluates Anthony's loan-to-value ratio. With a purchase price of $400,000 and a loan amount of $300,000, his LTV is 75%, which aligns with the stricter requirements for borrowers with credit challenges. This lower LTV reduces risk and strengthens his application.

Anthony has also built cash reserves of $25,000 after his down payment. With a monthly housing payment of $2,700, this provides approximately 9.3 months of reserves, exceeding the lender's requirement of six months. These reserves serve as an additional compensating factor.

To address his credit history, Anthony provides a letter of explanation detailing the circumstances that led to his past financial difficulties. He includes documentation showing the recovery of his business and consistent on-time payments over the past 18 months. This demonstrates that the issues were temporary and have been resolved.

Based on this analysis, the lender determines that Anthony's overall profile meets the requirements for approval. His strong income, low debt-to-income ratio, substantial down payment, and solid reserves offset the risk associated with his credit score. He is approved for the loan and able to purchase his home.

This example illustrates how self-employed borrowers with credit challenges can still qualify for a mortgage by leveraging compensating factors and presenting a strong financial profile. By focusing on income, managing debt, and addressing past issues proactively, borrowers can overcome obstacles and achieve their homeownership goals.

Chapter 10

Advanced Bank Statement Mortgage Loan Structuring

As you reach this final stage of the Bank Statement Mortgage Loan Mastery Series, it becomes clear that success in this space is not simply about qualifying—it is about engineering approvals. Advanced structuring is where strategy meets execution. It is the ability to take all the moving parts—income, deposits, expense ratios, credit, reserves, property type, and lender guidelines—and align them in a way that produces the strongest possible outcome. For self-employed borrowers, this is where the real advantage lies. You are not confined to a fixed paycheck or rigid documentation. You have the ability to shape your financial presentation, and when done correctly, this can unlock opportunities that traditional borrowers cannot access.

At the core of advanced structuring is the concept of optimization. Every element of your loan file can be adjusted, refined, or strategically positioned to improve your approval odds. This includes choosing the right type of bank statements, determining whether to use a 12-month or 24-month average, deciding between personal or business accounts, and evaluating whether a CPA-prepared profit and loss statement can enhance your income calculation. These decisions are not random—they are based on understanding how each option impacts the final numbers used by the lender.

One of the most powerful tools in advanced structuring is selecting the optimal income calculation method. For example, a borrower with increasing income may benefit from using a 12-month average rather than a 24-month average, as it captures more recent performance. Conversely, a borrower with fluctuating income may benefit from a longer averaging period to smooth out inconsistencies. Similarly, choosing between personal and business bank statements can significantly impact qualifying income. Personal statements may show higher usable income with fewer expense deductions, while business statements may require expense ratios that reduce qualifying income. Understanding which approach produces the best result is key.

Expense ratio optimization is another critical strategy. Lenders often apply standard expense ratios based on industry assumptions, but these ratios may not accurately reflect your actual business expenses. By providing a CPA-prepared profit and loss statement, you may be able to justify a lower expense ratio, increasing your qualifying income. For example, reducing an expense ratio from 50% to 35% can dramatically improve your income calculation. However, this must be done carefully and accurately, as inconsistencies between documents can create new challenges.

Deposit structuring is equally important. Not all deposits are treated equally, and how your income flows through your accounts can influence how it is interpreted. Ensuring that deposits are consistent, clearly identifiable as income, and supported by documentation helps maximize the amount that can be used for qualification. Avoiding unnecessary transfers, commingling, and irregular deposit patterns further strengthens your file. In advanced structuring, even small adjustments in how deposits are handled can lead to significant improvements in qualifying income.

Debt management plays a strategic role as well. Reducing or eliminating certain debts before applying can lower your debt-to-income ratio and increase your borrowing capacity. In some cases, paying off a small loan or reducing credit card balances can make the difference between approval and denial. Advanced structuring involves evaluating which debts have the greatest impact on your profile and addressing them proactively.

Reserves can also be used strategically. While meeting minimum reserve requirements is necessary, exceeding those requirements can serve as a powerful compensating factor. For example, having 12 months of reserves instead of the required six months can offset other weaknesses in your file, such as a higher debt-to-income ratio or lower credit score. Structuring your assets to demonstrate strong liquidity can enhance your overall application.

Another advanced strategy involves aligning your profile with the right lender. Not all lenders interpret guidelines in the same way. Some may offer more flexible expense ratios, higher allowable debt-to-income ratios, or different approaches to income calculation. Understanding these differences and selecting the lender that best fits your profile can significantly improve your chances of approval. This is where expertise and experience become invaluable.

Layering strategies is where advanced structuring truly comes together. Instead of relying on a single adjustment, multiple strategies are combined to create a stronger overall profile. For example, a borrower may use a 12-month average to capture higher income, apply a CPA-prepared P&L to reduce the expense ratio, pay down certain debts to lower the DTI, and maintain strong reserves to offset any remaining concerns. Each of these elements contributes to a more compelling application.

It is also important to think beyond the initial approval. Advanced structuring considers not only how to get approved but how to position yourself for future opportunities. This includes planning for refinancing, scaling investments, or improving loan terms over time. By structuring your loan with a long-term perspective, you can create a foundation for continued growth and financial flexibility.

Risk awareness remains a key component. While advanced structuring allows for optimization, it must be grounded in accuracy and compliance. Overstating income, misrepresenting deposits, or providing inconsistent documentation can lead to serious consequences. The goal is not to manipulate the system but to present your financial reality in the most effective and transparent way possible.

Ultimately, advanced bank statement mortgage loan structuring is about control. It is about understanding the rules of the system and using them to your advantage. As a self-employed borrower, you have the ability to shape your financial profile in ways that traditional borrowers cannot. By mastering these strategies, you can move beyond simply qualifying and begin engineering approvals that align with your goals. This chapter represents the culmination of everything you have learned, providing the tools to take your mortgage strategy to the highest level.

Real-Life Math Example: Engineering an Approval Through Advanced Structuring

Consider a self-employed borrower named Sophia, who owns an e-commerce business. Sophia is looking to purchase a home priced at $800,000. Her business generates strong revenue, but her financial profile requires careful structuring to maximize her qualifying income and meet lender requirements.

Sophia provides 24 months of bank statements showing total deposits of $720,000, averaging $30,000 per month. However, her income has increased significantly in the past year, with recent monthly deposits averaging $40,000. Using a 24-month average would result in a qualifying income of $15,000 per month after applying a 50% expense ratio. This would limit her borrowing capacity.

To optimize her profile, Sophia and her mortgage professional decide to use a 12-month average instead. Her total deposits over the past 12 months are $480,000, averaging $40,000 per month. Applying the same 50% expense ratio results in a qualifying income of $20,000 per month, a significant improvement over the 24-month calculation.

Next, Sophia works with her CPA to prepare a profit and loss statement that shows her actual expense ratio is closer to 35%.

Using this lower ratio, her qualifying income increases to $26,000 per month. This adjustment alone adds $6,000 in monthly qualifying income, greatly enhancing her borrowing capacity.

Sophia's existing monthly debts include a car payment of $800 and credit card payments of $600, totaling $1,400. She also has a small personal loan with a payment of $300. Before applying, she decides to pay off the personal loan, reducing her total monthly debt to $1,400.

The lender calculates her debt-to-income ratio based on her new qualifying income of $26,000. Sophia plans to make a 20% down payment of $160,000, resulting in a loan amount of $640,000. At an interest rate of 7.25%, her monthly principal and interest payment is approximately $4,370. Including taxes and insurance, her total housing payment is $5,200.

Adding her existing debt of $1,400 results in total monthly obligations of $6,600. Dividing this by her qualifying income of $26,000 produces a debt-to-income ratio of 25.4%, which is well within acceptable limits and provides a strong margin for approval.

Sophia also maintains cash reserves of $80,000 after her down payment. With a monthly housing payment of $5,200, this provides over 15 months of reserves, significantly exceeding lender requirements. Her credit score is 750, further strengthening her profile.

In addition to these strategies, Sophia ensures that her bank statements are clean and well-documented, with no unexplained deposits or irregularities. She provides supporting documentation for all major transactions and organizes her files in a clear and professional manner.

By combining multiple structuring strategies—using a 12-month average, applying a lower expense ratio, reducing debt, and maintaining strong reserves—Sophia transforms her financial profile. Her qualifying income increases from $15,000 to $26,000 per month, and her debt-to-income ratio drops significantly. These changes position her as a low-risk borrower despite the complexity of her income.

The lender reviews Sophia's application and approves the loan. Through advanced structuring, she is able to qualify for the home she wants while maintaining a strong financial position. This example illustrates how strategic adjustments across multiple areas can work together to create a successful outcome.

Sophia's case demonstrates that advanced structuring is not about a single change—it is about aligning every aspect of your financial profile to produce the best possible result. By understanding and applying these strategies, self-employed borrowers can move beyond limitations and achieve their real estate goals with precision and confidence.

Chapter 11

Building a Long-Term Strategy with Bank Statement Mortgage Loans

Reaching this stage of your journey means you are no longer just thinking about qualifying for a single mortgage—you are thinking in terms of strategy, leverage, and long-term positioning. For self-employed borrowers, bank statement mortgage loans are not simply a workaround for income documentation; they are a powerful financial tool that, when used correctly, can support a lifetime of wealth-building decisions. This chapter focuses on how to think beyond one transaction and begin building a repeatable, scalable strategy that aligns your business income, real estate goals, and financial future.

The first step in developing a long-term strategy is shifting your mindset from approval to positioning. Most borrowers approach a mortgage with a short-term goal: getting approved for a home or refinancing an existing property. While that is important, it is only the beginning. The real advantage comes from understanding how each loan fits into a broader financial plan. Every decision—how you structure your income, how much you put down, how you manage your reserves—affects not only your current loan but your ability to secure future financing. Strategic borrowers think several steps ahead.

Consistency becomes your greatest asset in long-term planning. Lenders value predictability, and the more consistent your financial profile is over time, the stronger your position becomes. This includes maintaining steady deposits, managing expenses effectively, and avoiding unnecessary disruptions in your financial records. For self-employed borrowers, this may require intentional planning, such as stabilizing income streams, maintaining organized accounts, and avoiding drastic changes in business operations before applying for financing. Consistency builds credibility, and credibility opens doors.

Another key component of long-term strategy is sequencing your loans. Not all loans should be approached at the same time or in the same way. For example, securing a primary residence with favorable terms may be the first step, followed by investment properties that build income and equity. Refinancing may come later, allowing you to access capital and reposition your portfolio. Understanding the order in which to pursue these opportunities can significantly impact your overall success. Strategic sequencing allows you to build momentum while minimizing risk.

Cash flow management is at the center of any long-term plan. Real estate is not just about ownership—it is about sustainable income. Ensuring that your properties generate positive or at least manageable cash flow is essential for maintaining financial stability. This includes evaluating rental income, expenses, and financing costs. For self-employed borrowers, aligning business income with property income creates a powerful combination that supports both personal and investment goals. The more effectively you manage cash flow, the more opportunities you can pursue.

Reserves should be viewed not as a requirement but as a strategic asset. While lenders require reserves to mitigate risk, having additional reserves provides flexibility and security. It allows you to handle unexpected expenses, take advantage of new opportunities, and maintain stability during periods of income fluctuation. Building and maintaining strong reserves should be a core part of your long-term strategy. It is not just about meeting minimum requirements—it is about creating a financial buffer that supports growth.

Credit management also plays a critical role over time. Even if you have successfully qualified for a loan, maintaining and improving your credit profile can lead to better opportunities in the future. This includes making payments on time, managing credit utilization, and avoiding unnecessary debt.

Strong credit enhances your ability to secure favorable terms, reduce costs, and access a wider range of loan programs. It is a long-term asset that should be actively managed.

Another important aspect is adaptability. The lending environment, market conditions, and your personal financial situation will all change over time. Interest rates may rise or fall, property values may fluctuate, and your business income may grow or evolve. A successful long-term strategy is not rigid—it adapts to these changes. This means staying informed, reassessing your position regularly, and being prepared to adjust your approach when necessary. Flexibility allows you to take advantage of opportunities as they arise.

Leveraging equity is a key strategy for growth. As you build equity in your properties, you gain access to additional capital that can be used for further investments or financial goals. This may involve refinancing, selling properties, or using other financing methods to unlock value. Understanding how to use equity effectively allows you to accelerate your progress and expand your portfolio. However, this must be done carefully to avoid over-leveraging and increasing risk.

Partnerships and professional relationships can also enhance your strategy. Working with experienced mortgage professionals, accountants, and real estate advisors provides access to knowledge and opportunities that may not be available otherwise. These relationships can help you navigate complex decisions, identify potential issues, and optimize your approach. Building a strong team is an investment in your long-term success.

It is also important to define your goals clearly. Whether your objective is homeownership, financial independence, portfolio growth, or business expansion, your mortgage strategy should align with those goals. Without a clear direction, it is easy to make decisions that do not support your long-term vision. By defining your objectives and aligning your actions accordingly, you create a roadmap for success.

Ultimately, building a long-term strategy with bank statement mortgage loans is about taking control of your financial future. It is about using the flexibility of these programs to create opportunities, manage risk, and achieve your goals. By thinking beyond individual transactions and focusing on the bigger picture, you can turn your income into a powerful tool for growth and stability. This chapter provides the framework for developing that strategy and moving forward with confidence.

Real-Life Math Example: Building a Long-Term Mortgage and Investment Strategy

Consider a self-employed borrower named Carlos, who owns a logistics company. Carlos has an average monthly deposit of $35,000, resulting in annual revenue of $420,000. Using a bank statement loan with a 50% expense ratio, his qualifying income is $17,500 per month. Carlos wants to build a long-term strategy that includes purchasing a primary residence and gradually expanding into investment properties.

Carlos begins by purchasing a primary residence priced at $600,000. He makes a 20% down payment of $120,000, resulting in a loan amount of $480,000. At an interest rate of 7%, his monthly principal and interest payment is approximately $3,200. Including taxes and insurance, his total housing payment is $3,800. His existing monthly debts total $1,200, bringing his total obligations to $5,000. Dividing this by his qualifying income of $17,500 results in a debt-to-income ratio of 28.6%, which is well within acceptable limits.

After securing his primary residence, Carlos focuses on building reserves and stabilizing his income. Over the next year, he maintains consistent deposits and increases his savings to $80,000. This positions him to pursue his next goal: purchasing an investment property.

Carlos identifies a rental property priced at $350,000. He makes a 25% down payment of $87,500, resulting in a loan amount of $262,500. The monthly payment, including taxes and insurance, is approximately $2,200. The property generates rental income of $2,800 per month, creating a positive cash flow of $600.

With the new property, Carlos's total monthly obligations increase to $7,200, including his primary residence and existing debts. Dividing this by his qualifying income of $17,500 results in a debt-to-income ratio of 41.1%, which remains within acceptable limits. His rental income further supports his ability to manage the additional debt.

Over time, the value of Carlos's investment property increases to $400,000. He decides to refinance at a 75% LTV, resulting in a new loan amount of $300,000. After paying off the existing balance of $250,000, he receives $50,000 in cash. He uses this cash, along with additional savings, to purchase a second investment property.

This second property follows a similar structure, generating rental income that exceeds its mortgage payment. As Carlos adds more properties, his rental income grows, creating additional cash flow and strengthening his overall financial position. His strategy focuses on maintaining positive cash flow, building equity, and using refinancing to fund future investments.

Throughout this process, Carlos maintains strong reserves and manages his credit carefully. His consistent income and disciplined approach allow him to continue qualifying for new loans. Over several years, he builds a portfolio of multiple properties, each contributing to his long-term financial goals.

This example demonstrates how a self-employed borrower can use bank statement mortgage loans as part of a broader strategy. By starting with a primary residence, building reserves, and gradually expanding into investment properties, Carlos creates a sustainable path to wealth. His approach highlights the importance of planning, consistency, and strategic decision-making.

By understanding how each step fits into a larger plan, self-employed borrowers can move beyond individual transactions and build a financial system that supports long-term success.

Chapter 12

Putting It All Together – Mastering Bank Statement Mortgage Loan Approvals

As you reach the final chapter of this series, everything you have learned begins to come together into a single, powerful framework. Bank statement mortgage loans are not just a niche solution—they are a complete system for self-employed borrowers to qualify, scale, and build long-term financial success. From understanding income to structuring deposits, reducing red flags, organizing documentation, leveraging equity, and planning strategically, each component plays a role in the final outcome. Mastery comes from integration. It is the ability to align every piece of your financial profile in a way that tells a clear, consistent, and compelling story to the lender.

The mortgage approval process is not random. It follows a structured evaluation of risk, and every part of your application contributes to that evaluation. Income determines capacity, credit reflects behavior, reserves demonstrate stability, and documentation provides verification. When any one of these elements is weak, the overall profile is affected.

When they are all aligned, the result is a strong and confident approval. This is why mastering bank statement loans is not about focusing on one area—it is about understanding how all areas work together.

At this level, preparation becomes your greatest advantage. Successful borrowers do not wait until they apply to think about their financial profile. They prepare in advance, structuring their income, organizing their accounts, and addressing potential issues before they arise. This proactive approach reduces uncertainty and positions you as a low-risk borrower. Preparation is not just about meeting requirements—it is about exceeding them in a way that strengthens your application.

Clarity remains a central theme. The easier it is for an underwriter to understand your income and financial situation, the more confident they will be in approving your loan. This means maintaining clean bank statements, providing complete documentation, and ensuring that all financial records are consistent. When your financial story is clear, the decision becomes easier for the lender. Complexity and confusion create hesitation, while simplicity and transparency create confidence.

Consistency over time is what transforms a one-time approval into a repeatable system. Lenders rely heavily on patterns, and the more consistent your income and financial behavior are, the stronger your profile becomes. This consistency allows you to move from one loan to the next with greater ease, building momentum and expanding your opportunities. It also reduces the need for extensive explanations, as your financial history speaks for itself.

Strategic thinking is what separates average borrowers from those who truly master this process. Instead of reacting to requirements, you anticipate them. You understand how changes in income, debt, or reserves will impact your profile, and you adjust accordingly. This level of awareness allows you to make informed decisions that align with your goals. Whether you are purchasing a home, refinancing, or investing, every move becomes part of a larger strategy.

Another key element is adaptability. The mortgage landscape is constantly evolving, and what works today may change in the future. Interest rates fluctuate, lending guidelines shift, and market conditions vary. A successful borrower remains flexible, adjusting their approach as needed. This may involve changing the timing of a loan, selecting a different program, or restructuring income to meet new requirements. Adaptability ensures that you remain in control, regardless of external changes.

Confidence is the result of mastery. When you understand how the system works and how to position yourself within it, you approach the process with clarity and purpose. This confidence is not based on guesswork—it is based on knowledge and preparation. It allows you to navigate challenges, make strategic decisions, and move forward with certainty. For self-employed borrowers, this confidence is especially valuable, as it transforms what can feel like a complex and uncertain process into a manageable and predictable one.

It is also important to recognize that this process is not just about getting approved—it is about building a financial foundation. Each loan you secure, each property you acquire, and each strategy you implement contributes to your long-term success. Bank statement mortgage loans provide the flexibility to align your financing with your actual income, allowing you to build wealth in a way that reflects your true financial capacity.

The lessons in this series are designed to empower you. They provide the knowledge and tools needed to take control of your financial future. Whether you are just starting or looking to scale your investments, the principles remain the same: clarity, consistency, strategy, and preparation. By applying these principles, you can move beyond limitations and create opportunities that align with your goals.

As you move forward, remember that mastery is an ongoing process. Each experience, each loan, and each decision adds to your understanding and strengthens your approach. The more you apply what you have learned, the more effective you become. Over time, what once seemed complex becomes second nature, and what once felt uncertain becomes predictable.

This final chapter represents not an ending, but a beginning. It is the starting point for applying everything you have learned and building a system that works for you. Bank statement mortgage loans are more than a solution—they are a strategy, a tool, and an opportunity. By mastering them, you take control of your financing, your investments, and your future.

Real-Life Math Example: Mastering the Full Strategy from Start to Scale

Consider a self-employed borrower named Elena, who owns a consulting business with consistent monthly deposits of $32,000, totaling $384,000 annually. Using a bank statement loan with a 50% expense ratio, her qualifying income is

$16,000 per month. Elena's goal is to build a long-term strategy that includes purchasing a primary residence, acquiring investment properties, and leveraging equity to scale her portfolio.

Elena begins by purchasing a primary residence priced at $500,000. She makes a 20% down payment of $100,000, resulting in a loan amount of $400,000. At an interest rate of 7%, her monthly principal and interest payment is approximately $2,660. Including taxes and insurance, her total housing payment is $3,200. Her existing monthly debts total $1,000, bringing her total obligations to $4,200. Dividing this by her qualifying income of $16,000 results in a debt-to-income ratio of 26.3%, which is well within acceptable limits.

After stabilizing her finances and building reserves of $60,000, Elena purchases her first investment property for $300,000. She makes a 25% down payment of $75,000, resulting in a loan amount of $225,000. The monthly payment is $1,900, and the property generates rental income of $2,500, producing a positive cash flow of $600.

With this addition, Elena's total monthly obligations increase to $6,100. Dividing this by her qualifying income of $16,000 results in a debt-to-income ratio of 38.1%, still within acceptable limits. Her rental income further supports her financial profile and demonstrates her ability to manage investment properties.

Over the next two years, the value of her investment property increases to $350,000. Elena refinances at a 75% LTV, resulting in a new loan amount of $262,500. After paying off the existing balance of $200,000, she receives $62,500 in cash. She uses this cash, along with additional savings, to purchase a second investment property.

This second property generates similar cash flow, adding another $600 per month to her income. As Elena continues this process, her portfolio grows, and her rental income increases. Each property contributes to her overall financial stability and provides additional opportunities for growth.

Throughout this journey, Elena maintains strong reserves, consistent income, and a disciplined approach to debt management. Her credit score improves over time, allowing her to secure better loan terms and reduce costs. By aligning her strategy with her financial goals, she creates a system that supports long-term success.

This example demonstrates how all the concepts in this series come together. By structuring income, managing debt, leveraging equity, and planning strategically, Elena transforms her financial profile into a powerful tool for growth. Her journey illustrates that mastery is not about a single transaction—it is about building a system that works over time.

By applying these principles, self-employed borrowers can move beyond limitations and create a path to financial independence. The strategies in this series provide the foundation for that journey, empowering you to take control of your future and achieve your goals with confidence.

Chapter 13

Creating a Repeatable System for Bank Statement Mortgage Success

At this stage, you are no longer just a borrower—you are becoming a system builder. The difference between those who occasionally qualify for a mortgage and those who consistently secure approvals, scale portfolios, and build lasting wealth is not luck or timing. It is the presence of a repeatable system. For self-employed individuals, this system is built around one core idea: aligning your income, documentation, and financial behavior in a way that consistently meets lender expectations. When this alignment becomes routine, mortgage approvals become predictable rather than uncertain.

A repeatable system begins with standardization. This means creating consistent processes for how you manage your income, deposits, expenses, and documentation. Instead of adjusting your finances only when you are preparing for a loan, you operate in a way that keeps you "approval-ready" at all times. Your bank accounts are clean and organized, your deposits are consistent and well-documented, and your financial records are always up to date. This eliminates the need for last-minute adjustments and allows you to move quickly when opportunities arise.

One of the most important components of this system is account structure. Maintaining separate business and personal accounts is not just a recommendation—it is a foundational principle. Your business account should clearly reflect revenue and operational expenses, while your personal account should show income distributions and personal spending. This separation creates clarity for underwriters and ensures that your income can be easily identified and calculated. Over time, this structure becomes second nature, making every future loan application smoother and more efficient.

Income consistency is another pillar of the system. While self-employed income may naturally fluctuate, the way it is deposited and presented can be controlled. Establishing regular billing cycles, maintaining predictable deposit patterns, and avoiding large gaps in income all contribute to a stronger financial profile. Even if your total income varies, consistency in how it is received and recorded builds confidence with lenders. This consistency becomes a key factor in repeat approvals.

Documentation management is where many borrowers fall short, but it is also where a repeatable system can provide the greatest advantage. Instead of scrambling to gather documents when applying for a loan, you maintain an organized and continuously updated set of records. This includes bank statements, profit and loss statements, invoices, contracts, and any other relevant documents. By keeping everything organized and accessible, you reduce delays, minimize errors, and present a professional and complete application every time.

Another critical element is ongoing financial monitoring. A repeatable system requires regular review of your financial profile to ensure that it remains aligned with lender expectations. This includes tracking your income trends, monitoring your debt levels, and maintaining sufficient reserves. By staying aware of your financial position, you can make adjustments as needed and avoid surprises during the application process. This proactive approach keeps you in control and allows you to respond quickly to opportunities.

Debt management becomes a strategic tool within this system. Instead of viewing debt as a fixed obligation, you actively manage it to optimize your profile. This may involve paying down certain balances, consolidating debts, or timing new obligations carefully. The goal is to maintain a debt-to-income ratio that supports your borrowing capacity while still allowing for growth. Over time, this disciplined approach to debt management enhances your ability to qualify for larger and more complex loans. Reserves are treated as a core component of the system rather than an afterthought. Maintaining strong reserves not only meets lender requirements but also provides flexibility and security. It allows you to pursue new opportunities, handle unexpected expenses, and demonstrate financial stability. By consistently building and maintaining reserves, you strengthen your profile and increase your ability to scale.

Another powerful aspect of a repeatable system is relationship building. Working with the same mortgage professionals, lenders, and financial advisors over time creates continuity and efficiency. These professionals become familiar with your financial profile, your goals, and your strategy, allowing them to provide more tailored guidance. Strong relationships can also lead to better opportunities, faster approvals, and more favorable terms.

Automation and simplicity are key to maintaining consistency. The more streamlined your processes are, the easier it becomes to sustain them over time. This may include setting up automatic transfers, using accounting software, or establishing routines for financial management. By reducing complexity, you make it easier to stay consistent and avoid errors.

A repeatable system also allows for scalability. As your income grows and your portfolio expands, the same principles can be applied at a larger scale. Whether you are managing one property or multiple investments, the system remains the same. This scalability is what enables long-term growth and success. It allows you to build momentum and continue expanding without losing control.

Ultimately, creating a repeatable system for bank statement mortgage success is about discipline and intentionality. It is about operating in a way that consistently aligns with your goals and the expectations of lenders. When this system is in place, you move from reacting to opportunities to creating them. You are no longer dependent on perfect timing or circumstances—you are prepared, positioned, and ready to act.

This chapter represents the evolution from learning to mastery. It is where knowledge becomes habit and strategy becomes routine. By implementing a repeatable system, you transform the mortgage process from a one-time event into a reliable and scalable part of your financial life.

Real-Life Math Example: Building a Repeatable Mortgage System for Ongoing Approvals

Consider a self-employed borrower named Victor, who owns a digital services business. Victor earns an average of $30,000 per month in deposits, totaling $360,000 annually. Using a bank statement loan with a 50% expense ratio, his qualifying income is $15,000 per month. Victor's goal is to create a repeatable system that allows him to qualify for multiple properties over time without needing to restructure his finances for each application.

Victor begins by organizing his accounts. He separates his business and personal finances, ensuring that all business income flows into his business account and that personal distributions are clearly documented. Over the next 12 months, his business account shows consistent monthly deposits of $30,000, all of which are easily identifiable as income. This consistency becomes the foundation of his system.

Victor's monthly debts include a car payment of $700 and credit card payments of $500, totaling $1,200. His initial debt-to-income ratio is 8%, providing significant room for additional borrowing. He purchases his first property, a primary residence priced at $500,000, with a 20% down payment of $100,000. The loan amount is $400,000, and his monthly housing payment is $3,200. His total monthly obligations increase to $4,400, resulting in a debt-to-income ratio of 29.3%.

After stabilizing his finances and building reserves of $50,000, Victor purchases his first investment property for $300,000.

He makes a 25% down payment of $75,000, resulting in a loan amount of $225,000. The monthly payment is $1,900, and the property generates rental income of $2,600, producing a positive cash flow of $700. Victor's total monthly obligations now increase to $6,300. Dividing this by his qualifying income of $15,000 results in a debt-to-income ratio of 42%, which remains within acceptable limits. His rental income further supports his profile and demonstrates his ability to manage multiple properties.

Because Victor has maintained a consistent financial system, his second loan application is significantly smoother than his first. His documentation is already organized, his income is consistent, and his financial profile aligns with lender expectations. This efficiency allows him to move quickly and take advantage of new opportunities.

Over time, Victor continues to follow the same system. He maintains consistent deposits, manages his debt strategically, and builds reserves. As his business grows, his monthly deposits increase to $40,000, raising his qualifying income to $20,000 per month. This increased income allows him to qualify for additional properties and expand his portfolio.

Victor also uses refinancing as part of his system. As his properties appreciate in value, he accesses equity to fund new investments. For example, if one of his properties increases in value from $300,000 to $360,000, he can refinance at a 75% LTV, resulting in a loan amount of $270,000. After paying off the existing balance of $225,000, he receives $45,000 in cash, which can be used toward his next purchase.

By repeating this process, Victor builds a portfolio of multiple properties, each contributing to his overall income and financial stability. His system allows him to move from one opportunity to the next with confidence and efficiency. Instead of starting from scratch each time, he relies on a proven structure that supports ongoing success.

This example demonstrates the power of a repeatable system. By maintaining consistency, organization, and strategic planning, self-employed borrowers can transform the mortgage process into a reliable and scalable tool for building wealth.

Chapter 14

Scaling to Financial Freedom Using Bank Statement Mortgage Strategies

At this level, the conversation shifts from qualification and structuring to something much bigger—scaling. Financial freedom is not achieved through a single loan or one successful transaction. It is built through a series of strategic decisions that compound over time. For self-employed borrowers, bank statement mortgage loans provide a unique advantage in this journey. They allow you to leverage your real income, not just what is reported on tax returns, creating opportunities to expand faster and more efficiently. This chapter is about taking everything you have learned and applying it at scale to build a system that produces long-term income, equity, and financial independence.

Scaling begins with a clear definition of your goal. Financial freedom means different things to different people. For some, it is the ability to cover all living expenses with passive income. For others, it is the flexibility to work on their own terms or to grow a business without financial pressure. Whatever your definition, your mortgage strategy must align with it. Real estate becomes a tool, not just an asset. Each property you acquire should move you closer to your objective, whether through cash flow, appreciation, or both.

One of the most important principles of scaling is leverage. Leverage allows you to control larger assets with a smaller amount of capital, amplifying your potential returns. Bank statement loans enable self-employed borrowers to access this leverage based on their true earning capacity. Instead of being limited by tax return income, you can qualify for larger loans and more properties. However, leverage must be used wisely. The goal is not to take on as much debt as possible, but to use debt strategically to create income and growth.

Cash flow becomes the foundation of financial freedom. While appreciation is important, it is not always predictable. Cash flow, on the other hand, provides consistent income that can be used to cover expenses, reinvest in new opportunities, and build reserves. When scaling, it is essential to focus on properties that generate positive cash flow or have a clear path to doing so. This ensures that your portfolio remains sustainable and does not become a financial burden.

Another key aspect of scaling is velocity—the speed at which you can move from one opportunity to the next. This is where your system, built in previous chapters, becomes critical. By maintaining consistent income, organized documentation, and strong financial metrics, you reduce the friction in the approval process. This allows you to act quickly when opportunities arise, whether it is purchasing a new property or refinancing an existing one. Speed, combined with strategy, creates momentum.

Portfolio diversification is also an important consideration. Relying on a single type of property or market can increase risk. By diversifying across different property types, locations, or income strategies, you create a more resilient portfolio. For example, combining long-term rentals with short-term rentals or investing in different markets can provide balance and reduce exposure to localized risks. Diversification strengthens your overall financial position and supports long-term stability.

Equity becomes a powerful tool as you scale. As your properties appreciate and your loan balances decrease, your equity grows. This equity can be accessed through refinancing or leveraged in other ways to fund additional investments. Understanding how to use equity effectively allows you to accelerate your growth without relying solely on new capital. However, it is important to balance equity extraction with maintaining sufficient ownership and stability in your portfolio.

Risk management remains essential at every stage of scaling. While the potential for growth increases, so does the complexity of your financial situation. Managing multiple properties, loans, and income streams requires discipline and careful planning. This includes maintaining adequate reserves, monitoring cash flow, and avoiding over-leverage. A well-managed portfolio is not just about growth—it is about sustainability.

Time is one of the most valuable assets in scaling. The earlier you begin implementing these strategies, the more time you have for compounding to work in your favor. Each property, each refinance, and each strategic decision builds on the previous one. Over time, this creates exponential growth. What may start as one or two properties can evolve into a significant portfolio that generates substantial income.

Another important factor is reinvestment. Instead of using all profits for personal expenses, reinvesting a portion into new opportunities accelerates growth. This may involve using rental income, business income, or refinance proceeds to acquire additional assets. Reinvestment is the engine that drives scaling, turning initial success into long-term wealth.

Mindset plays a crucial role in achieving financial freedom. Scaling requires patience, discipline, and a willingness to think long-term. There will be challenges, market fluctuations, and periods of uncertainty. However, by staying focused on your strategy and maintaining consistency, you can navigate these challenges and continue moving forward. Financial freedom is not achieved overnight—it is the result of sustained effort and strategic decision-making.

Ultimately, scaling with bank statement mortgage strategies is about creating a system that works for you. It is about aligning your income, your investments, and your goals in a way that produces consistent results. By leveraging your strengths as a self-employed borrower and applying the principles outlined in this series, you can build a path to financial freedom that is both achievable and sustainable.

Real-Life Math Example: Scaling a Portfolio to Achieve Financial Freedom

Consider a self-employed borrower named Marcus, who owns a consulting business with average monthly deposits of $40,000, totaling $480,000 annually. Using a bank statement loan with a 50% expense ratio, his qualifying income is $20,000 per month. Marcus's goal is to build a portfolio that generates enough cash flow to replace his active income.

Marcus begins by purchasing a primary residence for $600,000 with a 20% down payment of $120,000. His loan amount is $480,000, and his monthly housing payment is $3,800. His existing debts total $1,200, bringing his total obligations to $5,000. Dividing this by his qualifying income of $20,000 results in a debt-to-income ratio of 25%, leaving room for additional investments.

Marcus then purchases his first investment property for $350,000, making a 25% down payment of $87,500. The loan amount is $262,500, and the monthly payment is $2,200. The property generates rental income of $2,900, producing a positive cash flow of $700. His total monthly obligations increase to $7,200, resulting in a debt-to-income ratio of 36%.

Encouraged by this success, Marcus continues to acquire properties using the same strategy. Over the next three years, he purchases three additional properties, each generating approximately $600 to $800 in monthly cash flow. His portfolio now includes four investment properties with a combined monthly cash flow of approximately $2,800.

As property values increase, Marcus uses refinancing to access equity. For example, if one property increases in value from $350,000 to $420,000, he can refinance at a 75% LTV, resulting in a loan amount of $315,000. After paying off the existing balance of $250,000, he receives $65,000 in cash. He uses this cash to fund the down payment on another property.

By repeating this process, Marcus gradually expands his portfolio. After several years, he owns six investment properties generating a combined monthly cash flow of $4,500. Combined with his business income, this provides a strong financial foundation. As he continues to reinvest and scale, his cash flow increases further.

Eventually, Marcus reaches a point where his rental income covers his living expenses. At this stage, he has achieved financial freedom as defined by his goals. His portfolio continues to grow, providing both income and long-term appreciation.

This example demonstrates how scaling with bank statement mortgage strategies can lead to financial independence. By leveraging income, reinvesting profits, and using equity strategically, self-employed borrowers can build a portfolio that supports long-term success.

Chapter 15

Legacy Building and Long-Term Wealth Preservation Through Bank Statement Mortgage Strategies

As you arrive at this final chapter, the focus expands beyond income, approvals, and even scaling. Now, the conversation becomes about legacy—what you build, how you protect it, and how it continues to benefit you and those around you long after the initial work has been done. Bank statement mortgage strategies are not just tools for acquiring property or qualifying for loans; they are vehicles for creating long-term, generational wealth. For self-employed borrowers, this is a powerful realization. You are not just building income—you are building assets that can outlive your business, your career, and even your lifetime.

Legacy building begins with intentional ownership. Every property you acquire is more than a transaction; it is a long-term asset that has the potential to appreciate, generate income, and provide stability. Over time, these assets form a portfolio that represents years of strategic decisions and disciplined execution. The key is to approach each acquisition with a long-term perspective. Instead of focusing solely on immediate gains, consider how each property fits into your broader vision. Will it produce consistent cash flow? Is it located in an area with strong growth potential? Does it align with your overall portfolio strategy? These questions help ensure that your investments contribute to lasting value.

Preservation of wealth is just as important as its creation. As your portfolio grows, protecting it becomes a priority. This includes maintaining adequate insurance, managing debt responsibly, and ensuring that your properties are financially sustainable. Over-leveraging, neglecting reserves, or failing to monitor performance can put your assets at risk. A disciplined approach to risk management ensures that your portfolio remains stable even during periods of economic uncertainty. Preservation is not about avoiding growth—it is about ensuring that growth is sustainable.

Another critical aspect of legacy building is structuring ownership. As your portfolio expands, the way your assets are held can have significant implications for taxes, liability, and succession. Many investors choose to hold properties in business entities such as LLCs to provide a layer of protection and organization. Others may use trusts or other structures to facilitate the transfer of assets to future generations. While the specifics will depend on individual circumstances, the key is to think ahead and structure your portfolio in a way that supports your long-term goals.

Cash flow remains a central component of legacy wealth. Properties that generate consistent income provide not only financial security but also flexibility. This income can be reinvested, used to support your lifestyle, or allocated toward future opportunities. Over time, as loans are paid down and rents increase, cash flow typically improves, creating a compounding effect. This steady income stream is one of the most powerful aspects of real estate investing and a cornerstone of long-term wealth.

Debt, when used strategically, continues to play a role in legacy building. While reducing debt over time is important, leveraging debt to acquire assets can accelerate growth. The key is balance. As your portfolio matures, you may choose to pay down certain loans to increase cash flow and reduce risk, while maintaining leverage in other areas to support continued growth. This dynamic approach allows you to adapt to changing goals and market conditions.

Succession planning is an often-overlooked but essential part of legacy building. What happens to your assets when you are no longer managing them? Having a clear plan in place ensures that your portfolio can be transferred smoothly and continue to generate value. This may involve educating family members, establishing management structures, or working with professionals to create a formal succession plan. The goal is to ensure continuity and preserve the value you have built.

Tax efficiency also plays a significant role in preserving wealth. Real estate offers various tax advantages, including depreciation and potential deferral strategies. Understanding how to use these tools effectively can enhance your overall returns and reduce unnecessary tax burdens. While tax strategies can be complex, working with knowledgeable professionals can help you navigate these opportunities and integrate them into your long-term plan.

Another important element is adaptability across generations. The financial landscape will continue to evolve, and the strategies that work today may need to be adjusted in the future. Building a legacy means creating a system that can adapt and continue to perform over time. This includes maintaining flexibility in your portfolio, staying informed about market trends, and being open to new opportunities. A resilient portfolio is one that can withstand change and continue to grow.

Your mindset also evolves at this stage. The focus shifts from acquisition to stewardship. You are no longer just building wealth for yourself—you are managing it in a way that benefits others. This perspective encourages thoughtful decision-making and long-term planning. It also reinforces the importance of discipline, consistency, and strategic thinking.

Ultimately, legacy building through bank statement mortgage strategies is about creating something that lasts. It is about turning income into assets, assets into cash flow, and cash flow into lasting wealth. By combining the principles of acquisition, management, and preservation, you can build a portfolio that supports not only your goals but also the goals of future generations.

This chapter represents the culmination of your journey. It is where everything you have learned comes together to form a complete and enduring strategy. Bank statement mortgage loans are not just a means to an end—they are a foundation for building a legacy that stands the test of time.

Real-Life Math Example: Building and Preserving a Multi-Property Legacy Portfolio

Consider a self-employed borrower named Daniel, who owns a successful service business with average monthly deposits of $45,000, totaling $540,000 annually. Using a bank statement loan with a 50% expense ratio, his qualifying income is $22,500 per month. Daniel's goal is to build a portfolio that not only generates income during his lifetime but also serves as a legacy for his family. Daniel begins by acquiring a primary residence valued at $700,000 with a 20% down payment of $140,000. His loan amount is $560,000, and his monthly housing payment is $4,500. His existing debts total $1,500, bringing his total obligations to $6,000. Dividing this by his qualifying income of $22,500 results in a debt-to-income ratio of 26.7%, providing room for additional investments.

Over the next five years, Daniel acquires five investment properties, each priced around $400,000. For each property, he makes a 25% down payment of $100,000 and finances the remaining $300,000. Each property has a monthly payment of approximately $2,500 and generates rental income of $3,200, producing a positive cash flow of $700 per property.

With five properties, Daniel's total rental income is $16,000 per month, and his total mortgage payments for these properties are $12,500, resulting in a combined cash flow of $3,500. When combined with his business income, this creates a strong and diversified financial profile.

As property values increase, Daniel uses refinancing strategically. For example, if one property appreciates from $400,000 to $480,000, he can refinance at a 75% LTV, resulting in a loan amount of $360,000. After paying off the existing balance of $280,000, he receives $80,000 in cash. He uses these funds to invest in additional properties or to build reserves.

Over time, Daniel begins to shift his strategy toward preservation. He pays down certain loans to increase cash flow and reduce risk. For example, by paying off one property entirely, he eliminates a $2,500 monthly payment while retaining the full $3,200 rental income, increasing his net cash flow.

Daniel also establishes a trust to hold his properties, ensuring that they can be transferred smoothly to his family. He works with professionals to create a succession plan and educates his children on managing the portfolio. This ensures that the assets continue to generate income and value beyond his lifetime.

At this stage, Daniel's portfolio generates significant monthly cash flow, providing financial security and flexibility. His combination of business income and rental income creates a diversified and resilient financial structure. By maintaining strong reserves and managing his properties effectively, he preserves the value of his assets and positions them for continued growth.

This example illustrates how bank statement mortgage strategies can be used not only to build wealth but to preserve and transfer it. By combining acquisition, scaling, and long-term planning, self-employed borrowers can create a legacy that supports future generations and stands as a testament to disciplined and strategic financial management.

Final Thoughts

Your Path Forward with Bank Statement Mortgage Mastery

As you reach the end of this series, it is important to pause and recognize what you have gained. This is not just a collection of concepts about mortgages—it is a complete shift in how you understand financing as a self-employed borrower. You have moved from uncertainty to clarity, from limitation to opportunity, and from reacting to the system to learning how to work within it and ultimately master it. What once may have seemed confusing or restrictive now becomes a structured process that you can navigate with confidence.

The reality is that traditional mortgage systems were not built with self-employed individuals in mind. They were designed around predictable, salaried income, leaving entrepreneurs, business owners, and independent professionals at a disadvantage. But instead of accepting those limitations, you now understand that there are alternative paths—paths that align with how you actually earn, manage, and grow your income. Bank statement mortgage loans represent one of the most powerful of those paths, and through this series, you have learned how to use them effectively.

What makes this knowledge truly valuable is not just the ability to qualify for a loan—it is the ability to control the outcome. You now understand how income is evaluated, how deposits are analyzed, how expense ratios impact your numbers, and how documentation tells your financial story. These are not small details. They are the exact levers that determine whether a loan is approved, denied, or optimized. By understanding them, you move from being a passive participant in the process to becoming an active strategist.

This shift in control is what changes everything. Instead of asking, "Will I qualify?" you begin to ask, "How do I structure this to get approved?" That single change in mindset opens the door to endless possibilities. It allows you to approach each opportunity with intention and precision. Whether you are purchasing a home, refinancing, or building a portfolio, you are no longer guessing—you are planning.

Another key takeaway is that success in this space is not about perfection. It is about alignment. Your income does not need to be perfectly consistent, your credit does not need to be flawless, and your financial history does not need to be without challenges. What matters is how all the pieces come together. Strong income can offset weaker credit. Large reserves can offset higher debt ratios. Clear documentation can resolve uncertainty. When your profile is aligned correctly, approval becomes achievable. You have also learned that preparation is everything. The most successful borrowers do not wait until they apply to think about their finances—they operate in a way that keeps them ready at all times. Their accounts are organized, their deposits are consistent, their documentation is complete, and their financial profile is stable. This level of preparation reduces stress, eliminates surprises, and allows them to move quickly when opportunities arise.

Speed, in many ways, becomes an advantage. Real estate opportunities do not wait, and the ability to act quickly can make the difference between securing a deal and missing it. By maintaining a strong and consistent financial profile, you position yourself to take action without hesitation. You are not scrambling to gather documents or fix issues—you are ready.

Throughout this journey, one of the most important themes has been consistency. Not just in income, but in behavior. Consistent deposits, consistent account management, consistent documentation, and consistent financial discipline all contribute to a stronger profile over time. Consistency builds trust with lenders, and trust leads to approvals. Over time, this consistency compounds, making each subsequent loan easier than the last.

You have also seen how this process extends beyond a single transaction. A mortgage is not an isolated event—it is part of a larger financial strategy. Each loan you secure, each property you acquire, and each decision you make contributes to your long-term goals. Whether those goals involve homeownership, investment growth, financial independence, or legacy building, the principles remain the same. Structure, clarity, and strategy guide the way.

Another critical lesson is that leverage, when used correctly, can accelerate your progress. Bank statement loans allow you to leverage your real income, not just what is reported on paper. This opens the door to larger opportunities and faster growth. However, leverage must be balanced with discipline. The goal is not to take on unnecessary risk, but to use debt strategically to create income and build assets.

Risk management, therefore, becomes an essential part of the equation. Maintaining reserves, managing debt responsibly, and ensuring that your investments are sustainable all contribute to long-term success. Growth without stability is fragile. Stability without growth is limited. The balance between the two is where true success lies.

As you think about the future, it is important to recognize that the financial landscape will continue to evolve. Lending guidelines will change, markets will shift, and new opportunities will emerge. The principles you have learned in this series are not tied to a specific moment in time—they are adaptable. They provide a framework that can be applied regardless of external conditions. This adaptability ensures that you remain in control, no matter how the environment changes.

Your journey does not end here—it evolves. Each step you take builds on the last. Each loan, each property, and each decision adds to your experience and strengthens your understanding. Over time, what once required careful thought becomes second nature. You begin to see patterns, anticipate outcomes, and make decisions with greater confidence and speed.

It is also important to acknowledge that this process requires patience. Results may not happen overnight, but they do happen with consistency and effort. Financial success is built over time, through disciplined action and strategic thinking. The more consistently you apply what you have learned, the more predictable your results will become.

At its core, this series is about empowerment. It is about giving you the tools, knowledge, and perspective needed to take control of your financial future. As a self-employed borrower, you are not limited—you are simply operating within a different framework. Once you understand that framework, you can use it to your advantage.

You now have the ability to see opportunities where others see obstacles. You understand that income is not just what is reported—it is what can be demonstrated. You recognize that approval is not just about meeting requirements—it is about structuring your profile effectively. This perspective is what separates those who struggle from those who succeed.

As you move forward, carry this knowledge with you and apply it consistently. Continue to refine your approach, strengthen your financial profile, and align your actions with your goals. Stay disciplined, stay prepared, and stay focused on the long term. The path you are on is not just about mortgages—it is about building a system that supports your life, your ambitions, and your future.

In the end, the true value of what you have learned is not in any single strategy, but in the ability to think strategically. When you combine knowledge with action, you create results. When you apply those results consistently, you create momentum. And when that momentum is sustained over time, you create something far greater than a single approval—you create a future defined by opportunity, control, and lasting success.

How to Get a Personalized Bank Statement Mortgage Review

If you found this book helpful, you may want to see how these strategies apply to your specific financial situation.

Bank statement mortgage lending is highly customized—your deposits, income patterns, expense ratios, credit profile, property type, and long-term goals all play a role in determining what you qualify for and how your loan should be structured.

Every borrower's situation is different. The way your income flows through your accounts, how your business operates, your credit history, the property you are purchasing or refinancing, and current lender guidelines all impact your options. The strategies and examples in this book are designed to teach you how bank statement mortgage loans work—but your actual qualifying income, loan amount, and loan structure can only be determined by analyzing your real financial profile.

If you would like a no-obligation Bank Statement Mortgage review, you can request one here:

Email: info@FinibiMortgage.com

A licensed mortgage broker will review your bank statements, income structure, credit profile, and goals, and explain what bank statement mortgage options may be available to you—including:

• 12-month and 24-month bank statement programs• Personal vs business bank statement qualification• Primary residence and investment property financing• Cash-out refinance and equity access strategies• Advanced structuring to maximize qualifying income

No cost. No pressure. No obligation.

Sincerely,

Joseph G. Correa

Finibi Mortgage Inc.

Licensed Mortgage Broker

About the Author

Joseph G. Correa is a licensed mortgage broker and the founder of Finibi Mortgage, a Florida-based brokerage specializing in bank statement mortgage loans, non-QM lending, and strategic real estate financing solutions for self-employed borrowers, entrepreneurs, and investors.

With more than two decades of experience in mortgage lending, underwriting, and deal structuring, Joseph has helped thousands of clients qualify for real estate using alternative income documentation, unlocking opportunities that traditional lending often restricts.

Unlike traditional loan officers who rely strictly on tax returns and W-2 income, Joseph's approach focuses on real cash flow, income structuring, and financial strategy. He believes that borrowers should not be limited by how income is reported on paper, but instead empowered by how income is actually earned and managed.

Joseph is widely recognized for his expertise in:

• Bank statement mortgage loans• Self-employed borrower financing• Non-QM and alternative income lending• Investment property and portfolio financing• Cash-out refinance and equity strategies• Advanced mortgage loan structuring

Through his education platform, Finibi Academy, Joseph has trained tens of thousands of students worldwide in mortgage strategy, real estate investing, credit optimization, and financial independence.

He created the **Bank Statement Mortgage Loan Mastery Series** to provide a clear, step-by-step roadmap for borrowers and professionals who want to qualify for real estate without relying on traditional income documentation.

His mission is simple: To help people use their real income—not just their tax returns—to qualify, invest, and build long-term wealth.

When he is not structuring loans or writing, Joseph works with clients across the United States to design customized mortgage strategies that align with their financial goals, income structure, and long-term investment plans.

The Bank Statement Mortgage Loan Mastery Series Roadmap

The Complete Guide to Qualifying for Real Estate Using Bank Statements Instead of Tax Returns

The purpose of the **Bank Statement Mortgage Loan Mastery Series** is to give borrowers, investors, and mortgage professionals the exact strategies used by lenders and underwriters—translated into simple, practical steps you can apply in real life.

This series takes you from beginner to advanced mastery of how to qualify, structure, and scale real estate financing using bank statements instead of traditional income.

Each book builds on the last. You are not just learning how to get approved—you are learning how to control your approvals.

Book 1 — Bank Statement Mortgage Loan Fundamentals

Learn how bank statement loans work, how income is calculated, and why tax returns are no longer required for many borrowers.

Book 2 — Personal Bank Statement Mortgage Loans

Learn how to qualify using personal accounts, structure

deposits, and maximize usable income.

Book 3 — Business Bank Statement Mortgage Loans

Understand how lenders analyze business revenue, apply expense ratios, and use P&Ls.

Book 4 — Bank Statement Loans for Self-Employed Borrowers

Master how entrepreneurs qualify and structure income for approval.

Book 5 — Bank Statement Loans for Primary Residences

Learn how to buy or refinance your home using bank statement income.

Book 6 — Bank Statement Loans for Investment Properties

Discover how to scale rental portfolios using bank statement + DSCR strategies.

Book 7 — Jumbo Bank Statement Mortgage Loans

Learn how to finance high-value properties with advanced requirements and structuring.

Book 8 — Bank Statement Loan Refinancing & Cash-Out Strategies

Unlock equity, reduce payments, and reinvest capital using bank statement refinancing.

Book 9 — Bank Statement Loans with Credit Challenges

Learn how to qualify even with lower credit using compensating factors and strategy.

Book 10 — Advanced Bank Statement Mortgage Loan Structuring

Engineer approvals using deposits, expense ratios, and lender guidelines.

This series is designed to move you from understanding → execution → mastery.

By the end, you will not just know how to qualify—you will know how to structure deals like a professional.

Educational & Financial Disclaimer

The **Bank Statement Mortgage Loan Mastery Series** is intended for educational and informational purposes only.

This content is designed to help readers understand bank statement mortgage lending, real estate financing strategies, and income structuring concepts. It is not financial, legal, tax, or investment advice.

Joseph G. Correa and Live Stronger Faster are not acting as your personal financial advisor, attorney, accountant, or mortgage professional through this publication.

Mortgage guidelines, underwriting standards, interest rates, and loan programs vary by lender and may change at any time without notice.

All examples in this series are for illustration purposes only and do not guarantee approval or results.

Always consult with licensed professionals before making financial decisions.

Risk Disclosure

Bank statement mortgage lending and real estate investing involve risk.

Income fluctuations, interest rate changes, market conditions, and lender guidelines can all impact loan approval and financial outcomes.

Borrowing against real estate or using leverage increases both potential returns and risks.

Failure to repay a loan may result in foreclosure and loss of property.

Cash flow, rental income, and appreciation are not guaranteed.

All strategies in this series are educational and must be evaluated based on your individual financial situation.

You are solely responsible for your financial decisions.

www.ingramcontent.com/pod-product-compliance
Ingram Content Group UK Ltd.
Pitfield, Milton Keynes, MK11 3LW, UK
UKHW020159290926
15471UKWH00005B/950

9 798295 813597